PRIVATE LENDER
PLAYBOOK

How to Passively Invest in Real Estate
as a Private Mortgage Lender

PRIVATE LENDER PLAYBOOK

How to Passively Invest in Real Estate as a Private Mortgage Lender

Brant Phillips
with Nathan Long

Ainsley&Allen
PUBLISHING

ISBN-10: 1-946694-18-5
ISBN-13: 978-1-946694-18-8

A portion of royalties from the Retail Sales of "Private Lender Playbook" are donated to the Houston Area Parkinson Society (HAPS).

HOUSTON
AREA
PARKINSON
SOCIETY

The mission of the Houston Area Parkinson Society is to improve the quality of life for those affected by Parkinson's disease through services, education and advocacy.

Founded in 1974, HAPS is one of the oldest independent, local Parkinson's disease social service organizations in the United States. HAPS provides comprehensive services to eight counties in metropolitan Houston, with an estimated population of more than 6 million people.

HAPS offers numerous programs and services to the Parkinson's community. Over 40 weekly exercise, water, music and speech therapy groups in addition to tai chi, tango, yoga, dance, singing and non-contact boxing classes are made available by HAPS free of charge.

Professionally facilitated support groups are offered at no cost to individuals living with Parkinson's and their caregivers to share their experiences in a warm, friendly environment. In addition, HAPS offers free transportation services to and from HAPS programs and physician visits. Social services, respite, emergency financial aid, education programs and a monthly newsletter are also available.

You can learn more about Houston Area Parkinson Society (HAPS) by visiting www.hapsonline.org.

"I have been a real estate lender for many years, and have made many loans to Brant Phillips or some of his coaching students. I can honestly say that this book is not only invaluable to new real estate lenders, but it can also teach experienced lenders some things as well. Kudos to Brant for spending the time to lay all pieces out in a clear and conscientious way."

– Bill T.

"My old grandfather always said "never a borrower nor a lender be". I think that even he would feel more comfortable about lending private money for real estate after reading this book. Brant systematically lays out the full picture of the private money landscape and highlights the potential risks as well as the significant upside. Having worked with Brant for over 8 years and having loaned private money myself to his company and to others on multiple projects, I can tell you he nailed it with this book. A must read if considering deploying funds in this way."

– Karen W.

"I wish this book had been available when beginning my real estate quest! Brant has compiled a valuable resource that should be included in any real estate investor's library of reference books."

– Paul N.

"We began working with Brant many years ago through his coaching program and that's when we first learned about the private money lending side of the investing business. Since then we have rapidly grown our investing business thanks in part to our private lending relationships. It's been an absolute joy helping our private lenders to grow their retirement and wealth while at the same time growing our own real estate investing business. We can wholeheartedly attest to the character and integrity of Brant and to the fact that the methods shared in this book absolutely work!"

– Stephen & Shelley L.

ॐ ॐ

"As my wife and I began acquiring distressed homes to rehab into rental properties, we met Brant Phillips many years ago. Working with Brant on our rental homes enabled us to get to know him. We have seen firsthand his work ethic, professionalism and integrity, thereby making the transition to private lending with Brant seamless."

– Don O.

Acknowledgements

I started in this business as a young entrepreneur with nothing more than a dream and a drive to become a successful real estate investor to achieve financial freedom and experience more of the American dream. Never in my mind would I have imagined the journey that I've been on! It's been an incredible ride so far, and there have been a countless number of incredible people that have helped me to live out my dream.

To my family, friends, associates, employees, and certainly to all of my private lenders and those who have supported me, followed me and encouraged me along the way, I extend my deepest appreciation and honor to each and every one of you.

The entrepreneurial journey continues…

Table of Contents

Preface – We found a better way
by Ron & Ann M.

I retired in 2008. Stock market losses ate 50% of my life savings. Hang in there for five or six years to hopefully break even without touching one penny for withdrawals? Wait for the next "buying opportunity?" No thanks, there has to be a better way.

I round up the usual suspects: bank CD's, annuities, ETF's; all with risk vs. reward. Maybe Hedge funds! No, I'm a few million short of qualifying. Like Goldilocks, one is too hot, one too cold, none just right.

CD's at 0.5% double my money in a mere 150 years – too cold! Annuities confiscate my money forever; eat up 7% invested on day one, and drizzle back 4% until I die-still too cold. ETF's put me back in the market- with only 7,000 fund choices - plus a high sleepless night quotient- too hot for me.

I pause to think: Why can't I be like the banker in my childhood home town? All he did was loan out the bank's cash for interest, mostly for home mortgages. My folks got one of his mortgages for $14,500 back in the day. That banker lived in the biggest house, drove the fanciest car, built the most impressive marble building, walked on the deepest carpet and sat behind the largest mahogany desk made.

Here I am in 2008 looking for someone successful so I can do what they do. It hits me that what was old is new. The banker made thousands just on my folk's loan. His risk was minimal. He'd done his homework. Worst case he'd get a fine house back. He doubled the banks money while collecting a payment each month, all for lending to responsible people. This strikes me as just right.

My search leads me to self-directed IRA firms letting me make loans using my IRA cash. Loans like the banker did, only this time I'll be the one to double my money. I kiss a few frogs and then find Quest IRA just miles from me. We have since done 40+ loans using them.

We needed a responsible person(s) to loan to. At a Quest mixer we meet Brant Phillips and do our due diligence. Our assessment was that he has the highest level of integrity and operates from a win -win basis. This has never wavered in our 10 years of doing business together during scores of loans. If Brant tells you it's so, you can take it to the bank–and we have.

We have found the better way. Several examples in this book are our loans. They provide a steady stream of "mailbox money". We sleep well knowing our cash plus interest will return to us, all secured by homes. Homes that working families live in; quality properties where local neighborhoods are improved. We help Brant, his family and people be well provided for. No Annuity or ETF match can match that.

Is there a learning curve to know the steps in loaning your money? Yes. Is there paperwork involved? Yes. Good carpenters say, measure twice, saw once. My advice, read this book twice. Know you are in good hands. You have found the person who is successful; do what he does- it's all in this book!

When you have a big enough why, the how becomes small. We just returned from three weeks in Hawaii and have our next Costa Rica trip set, thanks to those interest checks. As can you. We encourage you to take action.

Introduction

I was introduced to the concept of private mortgage lending in early 2009 during the midst of the mortgage 'meltdown' and one of the greatest financial crashes the world has ever seen. The masses were running from the stock market and real estate at the same time. For those of you who were invested during this time, you know firsthand the financial carnage this era brought upon many, if not most. Stocks were volatile like never before and real estate values sunk like an anchor overboard. I've heard economists call the maiden decade of the 21st Century as the "lost decade", and for good reason. It began with the tragedy of 9/11 during a financial bear market brought on by the tech bubble, By the end of the decade we were in the thick of the "great recession" and the financial collapse.

This book is birthed from that era.

You see, in 2007 I decided to become a real estate investor. Great timing, right? Add to the mix, I knew nothing about real estate and had no business experience whatsoever. My wife and I were living in an apartment and starting a family. We had one child at the time and another on the way. After serving seven years in law enforcement after college, I decided the grass would certainly be greener in corporate America. So I left my career as a police officer, with a rank of sergeant, and traded in my badge and gun for the corporate world. I quickly realized that I was wrong, the corporate world was not for me.

However, I vowed to my wife to work hard at my job until I could find another avenue to pursue. And I did. I excelled in the corporate world and consistently finished at or near the top in my area for sales growth and was loyal and hardworking for my company. But I was looking for a 'better way' to provide for my family and one that would give me something more meaningful to pursue. So after much reading, research and soul searching, my sights became focused on the world of real estate and becoming a real estate investor. Did I mention that we had no money either?

In late 2006, my wife and I had just finished paying off our college loans and other miscellaneous debt, which put us ahead of many of our peers. However, as a couple in our late twenties, other than a dream and a drive to succeed, that was about it. And while I lacked experience and cash, I did have excellent credit, and that would be the impetus to help get this dream off the ground.

So with a dream, a drive and a 700+ credit score, I leveraged my way in 2007 to buy ten investment properties, all rentals and did so while continuing to work my full-time job. I used a 0% interest credit card to borrow money to put down on the first property, then used creative real estate strategies to buy the next nine. By the end of the year, I had acquired ten cash-flowing properties that I was also able to refinance with long-term financing with the banks. The rest as they say was history. Not really, the fun was only about to begin.

In 2008, as we all know, things began to change drastically in the real estate and credit markets. The company I was working for had a massive layoff to start the year. I was not one of the casualties, but that experience helped solidify my resolve to not be dependent upon others to provide for my family, and so my focus on investing continued to grow. However, I could no longer obtain bank financing to finance any additional properties. I was essentially at a dead end in my business, or so I thought.

I began telling close friends, family members and associates about my real estate pursuits in hopes of finding potential partners so I could continue to purchase investment properties. That year, while still working my corporate job, I purchased another ten rental properties with the help of three different partnerships. All in all, 2008 was a success. However I soon realized that partnerships with 50% splits going to my partners was going to delay my being able to reach my goal to escape the 'rat race' of corporate America and the financial freedom I desired. I wanted to be my own boss and have more time to spend with my family. I wanted to pursue real estate investing full-time and I wanted my version of the American dream! Unfortunately, 2009 was quickly approaching and I still had the same problem I had when I began 2008, which was being able to get financing for my properties. While the country was experiencing a massive financial crisis, real estate was on sale, but I was experiencing a financing crisis!

In December of 2008, equipped with an edition of Real Estate Investor Magazine, a friend and I met for a breakfast mastermind to discuss our investing goals for 2009. Turns out in hindsight, that 2009 was an incredible year to buy real estate! The only problem was, without financing, it didn't matter how cheap we could find properties for if we didn't have the ability to get them closed and funded. The answer to my problem was quickly revealed in that magazine during our breakfast meeting. I could sense things were about to change that day when I first learned about private mortgage lending.

It was a 'light bulb' moment for me I will never forget. Not only did private mortgage lending provide a way to fund my investing pursuits so I could continue to grow my business and leave my job, but I soon discovered this was an absolute incredible investment opportunity for my lenders as well. I instantly realized I had found something that would not only help me to grow my investing business, but at the same time, it would provide my lenders with an excellent investment opportunity. This was the epitome of a 'win-win' deal and then some!

Private mortgage lending would not only allow the lender to earn above market rates of return, but it was doing so with an investment that was secured by real estate and contained equity. To make things even better, their investment was going to help restore and revitalize our neighborhoods and employ local contractors and trades. It was providing my lenders something they desperately needed at the time and still do, which is predictable and steady returns in an otherwise unstable market. They were able to avoid the ups and downs of the stock market with an investment that would be secured by the real estate I was buying, with significant amounts of equity, while also receiving passive income and returns without sending their hard earned capital to Wall Street. Instead, they invested securely in their own backyard. In the proverbial battle of Wall Street versus Main Street, in I think you'll find when it comes to private mortgage lending playing the part of Main Street, Main Street wins in a cake walk.

Since 2009, I've gone on to invest in hundreds of deals funded by my private lenders and I'm proud to say with a 100% track record. This doesn't mean that I haven't lost money on any of my deals, because I absolutely have, but what it means is my lenders have never lost any of their capital and they've earned every single dollar I've promised to pay them as outlined in our loan documents. That's right, even when I've lost money on a few deals here and there, my lender's returns have been exactly what they were promised as stated in their loan documents. I don't think you'll find that on Wall Street!

Since I've discovered the world of private mortgage lending, I've been able to successfully grow my investment portfolio and live out my entrepreneurial dreams, in thanks and large part, to my private lenders, whom I also call my friends. We've grown together over the years and often talk about how happy and grateful we are for one another. They help me, and I help them. My lenders continually reinvest their capital in our deals and refer many others to us. Our lenders have grown organically from word of mouth and repeat clients, and they all think it's the greatest thing since sliced bread. Hey, that's their words, not mine! As I've grown my businesses, I often get invited to speak at various events and seminars, and I'm always shocked at how few people even realize the opportunity that private mortgage lending provides. The Book of Proverbs says we should "not withhold good from those who deserve it when it is in our power to act", so I decided to write this book so I could share with others about this opportunity. I'm extremely excited about the idea of helping others learn what my lenders and I have been successfully doing for years. This book is a way to give back, and help others. Hopefully you can see the power that is available by investing in real estate mortgages as a lender, while letting others do all the work. Perhaps most importantly, no longer feeling dependent upon the volatile and untrusting stock market.

This is not to say that private mortgage lending is 100% safe, because it is absolutely not! There is nothing 100% safe nor guaranteed about any investing opportunity and this strategy is no exception. However, with some basic principles and fundamentals applied, you can greatly improve your success ratio. This book is about sharing my experiences through hundreds of real estate deals as an investor and also as a lender (yes, I'm also a lender myself these days), to provide you with a blueprint, a playbook if you will, to help you construct your private lending roadmap.

I believe this book can be an empowering starter kit to help you lay the foundation of a private mortgage investment strategy that can provide you with many years, if not decades of solid and steady returns if done wisely. I believe you'll find new insights and opportunities you may not have even known existed. I will also cover many of the common lending myths and pitfalls I have seen and dispel some of the misconceptions that are also floating around.

My aim is to provide this content in a simplified manner which is easy to digest and easy to execute. Moreover, although simplified, I will give you some amazing and powerful wealth enhancement strategies covered in detail, and by the end of the book, you will be equipped to begin to pursue returns as a private mortgage lender starting immediately.

I would like you to consider that after reading each chapter you take a moment to reflect on the greatest insights that came to you and also to take notes in the space provided on the specific actions that you feel are pertinent for you. Taking this time to reflect and write some action items down will help to cement your thoughts and establish a plan to take action. As we all know, the results we desire will never occur unless the appropriate actions are taken. I encourage you to take on an 'Active' mindset as you read through this book so that you can build a investment strategy that is extremely passive for you and your portfolio.

Also, be sure to take notice of the informational website links that are provided in the book to further increase your knowledge and understanding of this wealth building strategy. I'm sure you'll find valuable content from the suggestions provided in the book.

Lastly, I would like to say that I'm not an attorney, an accountant, or a certified financial advisor. Nor am I offering any security or an opportunity to invest with me or any of my companies. And most assuredly, I'm not telling anyone that private mortgage lending is easy, safe, guaranteed or some type of get rich quick scheme. I would be lying if I did so and I would never jeopardize my name and my reputation that I've worked hard for! Rather, the intent of the Private Lender

Playbook is to equip you with the knowledge you need in order to create similar strategies that my lenders and other incredibly successful and wealthy private mortgage lenders have used for decades. You will learn how to 'be like the bank' and never feel dependent upon Wall Street again. You will also discover how to develop a perpetual investment strategy that can create a meaningful transformation not only for your wealth, but to the communities that you invest in. Welcome to the Private Lender Playbook and your exciting investing future!

Chapter 1: What is Private Mortgage Lending?

"The more you learn, the more you earn"

– Frank Clark

If you are reading this book then you probably already know investing in real estate is one of the most popular and widely used strategies to generate passive income and build wealth. But maybe you don't have the time or desire to own rental properties or to flip homes. Or, maybe you are already doing that but want to explore new ways to re-invest your money into the real estate market. Private mortgage lending provides a great opportunity for those who want to invest in real estate without getting their hands dirty.

Many of the people I talk to who are just getting started are under the false assumption that private lending is only for experienced lenders or for multi-millionaires that have money to spare. But the truth is, many of the private mortgage lenders I've worked with were actually first-time lenders who had never done a deal before. What is just as important to note is many of these private lenders started with $100,000 or less to invest.

Within this book, I hope to equip you with an overview and insight into an incredible investment opportunity that is available to you. I also want to dispel some misconceptions that people have about private mortgage lending. In order to do that, I will first give a quick overview of what private mortgage lending is. This will allow you to have a better understanding as we move forward and dig a little deeper into the process.

WHAT IS PRIVATE MORTGAGE LENDING?

Private Mortgage Lending is a process that occurs when a private money lender makes a loan to a real estate investor to purchase real estate, typically for short-term loans. This is also called a private mortgage and is also known as creating a Note, or sometimes referred to as trust deed investing. With a private mortgage, private lenders are basically assuming the role of the bank. Instead of the real estate investor borrowing from a traditional lender, they borrow from another person, which we will refer to as a Private Lender or Private Mortgage Lender (PML). The concept of a private money loan is relatively simple. There are three elements that are required for this type of loan: a borrower, a lender and the proper paperwork. I'll dive a bit deeper into how to analyze a buyer and go over all the necessary paperwork in later chapters. In the context of this book, the focus will be on single family home real estate investments.

I also want to stress that private mortgage loans are not "subprime" mortgages and made with false projections or derivatives. Private mortgage loans, when done correctly, are based on the value of the asset right now, not future projections based on appreciation. The most successful lenders that I've seen in this industry are those who invest in conservative deals with verified numbers and ratios and they stick to their guns and don't fall into the trap of speculation and gambling on deals with borrowers. These investments should be high-yield, income producing, low-risk investments that greatly improve your investment portfolio, and peace of mind.

While a private money lender serves the same purpose as a traditional lending institution, there are several key differences. One major difference is that private money lenders will typically charge higher rates than banks. However, they are also more likely to make loans that the average bank would usually pass on. This makes private mortgage loans an attractive option for many real estate investors who need to find alternatives to the traditional bank loan. It is also important to note that private lenders can offer benefits that traditional lenders cannot offer to real estate investors. While banks and similar lenders can typically offer the most attractive rates, they do not provide the same combination of speed and transparency in the decision-making process as does a private lender. I will go a little bit further into these points later on in the book.

Private mortgage lending is also very similar to hard money loans. If you're new to the world of real estate investing, you'll learn a little bit more about hard money loans in upcoming chapters. In a nutshell, hard money lenders (HMLs), as we will refer to them in this book, will issue loans on real estate deals that need a lot of work in repairs. Many banks will not finance these homes. Hard money lenders have the ability to provide a quick closing for the real estate investor. HMLs are extremely useful for investors and those who are having a hard time getting approved for a bank loan or those who need to close quickly. However hard money loans are often much more expensive than other mortgages and require low loan to value ratios.

The obvious question comes down to this: is private mortgage lending safe in today's market? While much has been learned from the mortgage meltdown from the past, which resulted in the big banks and lending institutions revamping their lending guidelines, in today's market, private mortgage lending is actually rated as one of the most preferred types of investments available on the market, simply because the loan is secured by real estate. So unlike most other investments, if the unfortunate event occurs and the borrower defaults, you are not left holding nothing, but instead have the opportunity to take possession of the asset to either sell, rent, or seek other ways to generate income from your investment. In other words, your investment is secured by the piece of real estate that you loaned on.

Ultimately, the goal of private mortgage lending is to create a win-win solution whereby everybody gains financially while minimizing risk. In fact, like I briefly mentioned before, when the loans are structured properly and the private lender does the proper due diligence prior to making the loan, the lender should come out ahead financially if something were to go 'wrong' with a deal. Therefore, it is essential to always perform the proper due diligence and have the proper documentation in place, prepared by a real estate attorney. Consequently, if any issues arise, any payments and fees you have received from the investor are yours to keep. Moreover, you can also take possession of the house if your investor defaults on the loan, which typically leaves you with 20 to

30% equity in the property that you can profit from. Much more to come on this later.

Chapter Takeaways

Always remember that a private mortgage loan is an investment. Meaning there will always be risks so you need to do your homework to ensure that the deal is viable. That being said, private mortgage lending is widely viewed as one of the safest and most preferred types of investments available on the market, because it is a security backed investment that provides the investor a peace of mind that many other investments cannot provide.

Though you should certainly analyze your options before entering into a deal, don't let the risks hold you back from reaping the rewards of this powerful investment opportunity. Remember that the most successful lenders are those who invest in deals that meet their criteria and their lending guidelines. Establish conservative guidelines for yourself based on lending standards that have been proven to work and stick to your guns in order to produce the results many others are receiving in today's market. Remember, when done correctly, private mortgage lending should be a high-yield, income producing, low-risk investment that you can enjoy investing in for years to come.

Chapter 2: Why not the Banks?

"Necessity is the mother of invention"

– Ancient Proverb

The world is full of banks and lending institutions. So you might be wondering, why don't real estate investors just borrow from a bank? In reality, it is not that simple for many investors. There are a few common challenges or circumstances that can hold back a potential real estate investor from getting the money they need, even if they are completely capable of managing a successful deal and paying back the lender. In this chapter, I will discuss a few scenarios that explain why bank loans are not ideal for real estate investors and why private mortgage lending presents a better opportunity for real estate investors instead of a traditional lending institution like a bank.

TIME

The most common reason investors seek private money is because they simply do not have the luxury of time it takes to go through the lending process to get a bank loan. The application process can be lengthy, and even after it's finished, the borrower has to wait, sometimes for weeks, to hear back about whether or not they were approved. The real estate investment market often moves quickly and investors need to move fast on properties as they do not have the luxury of waiting on the bank.

In many instances, when a real estate investor like myself goes under contract to purchase a home from a motivated seller, closing on the home may occur within a week and sometimes even quicker. There simply is not enough time to go through an entire loan process with a bank, because even in the best case scenario, the bank loan process takes 3-4 weeks. In reality, most banks take even longer to process applications, much less to fully fund a loan request.

I know this because I still utilize the banks to fund many of my deals, but I use them for essentially two types of financing: Construction Loans and Long Term Financing for Rental Properties. For both of these types of deals, urgency usually isn't an issue, so time is on our side. But for a majority of the deals we do, banks simply are not a viable option for us when we are required to close quickly. In this regard, private money lenders certainly help fill a specific need in the marketplace for investors like myself.

NOT QUALIFIED

Another reason many real estate investors do not borrow from a traditional lender is because the investor or the type of property they are purchasing may not qualify for a traditional bank loan or construction loan. This is especially true if the investor is relatively new to the industry and has not had the chance to show they can be successful. No matter how hard the new investors have worked to understand the industry and learn the proper processes, many banks are just not willing to take a chance on those who do not have extensive experience, a history of successful deals and more importantly, a strong personal financial statement.

You see, banks analyze and value the strength of the borrower more than the numbers of the deal. Conversely, private mortgage lending is often called 'asset based lending' because what is most important to private lenders is the actual asset itself. With asset based lending, the real estate investor, whether a newbie or not, has the ability to land a home-run deal. Private lenders will gladly loan to an investor if there is enough equity and security in the deal itself. Of course, private lenders will factor into the equation the skill, experience and character of their borrower/investor, but they analyze the property first. Therefore, the lack of experience or even poor financials of the borrower is not an automatic disqualifier. This is a tremendous value private money lenders bring to the marketplace that banks fail to do.

Let's face it, there are a multitude of new real estate investors continuously entering into the market trying to get into the real estate investing industry and many of the newcomers are on a shoestring budget, to say the least. This means they are not financially capable of getting approved for bank financing on investment properties that are deemed much riskier than standard loans. I know, because this was how I got started in the business.

As you learned in the introduction of this book, I used a credit card to help with the down payment for my first investment property. When I decided to begin real estate investing. My wife and I had just finished paying off our student loans and a few other bills we accrued from our wedding and miscellaneous expenses. Fortunately, I have always maintained a strong credit score, so I used that strong credit score to my advantage and leveraged it to purchase my very first investment property. You may find a lot of new investors that you come across are like me 10+ years ago. I was young, motivated, and extremely driven to achieve success. However, on paper, when it came down to my financials, I posed a risk to the banks as I was extremely "wet behind the ears" and under-funded. I couldn't blame them. It was then I turned to non-conventional means for financing (Hard Money Loans). Looking back now, 10+ years and hundreds of successful deals later, I am happy to say that I have proven the banks wrong, however, I understand their lending criteria. Which also means I understand the deficiencies and flaws within their system in relation to the business of investing.

BANKS DON'T LIKE "UGLY" HOUSES

As I mentioned earlier, banks view many investment properties as 'high risk' loans due to the condition of the properties that real estate investors tend to buy. Many investors specialize in purchasing "ugly" houses they intend to rehab and flip or hold as rental properties. Even if the investor has extensive and well thought out plans to renovate a property that is in poor condition, banks typically don't want to extend loans to borrowers buying these ugly houses. Banks have plenty of loan applications for "pretty" houses that are owner occupied. Let's face it, "pretty" houses are safer loans for them to make, especially when they will be occupied by the homeowner. These are simply the facts.

Ugly house deals cause the banks to get bogged down in their policies, procedures and guidelines preventing them from lending on deals by not taking into account the amount of equity in the property and by not considering the experience of the borrowers. So much so, that many banks, and Wall Street as well, in the form of hedge funds, are beginning to admit the error in their thinking and lean more towards lending more freely on investment deals that meet basic asset based lending criteria, which I will cover later in this book. However, in my opinion, it's too little and a little too late. The private mortgage lending community has risen up to fill the void and has done so with flying colors!

BANKS DON'T LIKE SMALL LOANS

Another point to take into consideration is that many real estate investors like to invest in deals that are less than $100,000 total investment. Many of the deals in the Texas market are in the $50,000 - $75,000 range. Yes, you read it correctly, many of the deals that investors in our market purchase are a total investment of less than $75,000 and the banks do not like these loans. As a matter of fact, I'm currently investing in the East Texas market and we are buying homes in the $15,000 - $25,000 range! These types of properties are a great lending opportunity for private money lenders with a limited amount of capital or who simply have other capital tied up in other deals. This small loan type gives the lender an opportunity to put their money to work, still secured in real estate and earning a very nice return. And the best part is, the banks don't want to lend on these deals simply because they are too small and not worth their time which means less competition for you as a private lender!

TOO MUCH PAPERWORK

Another thing to consider is that banks and other traditional lenders require a lot of documentation throughout the application and loan process. As crazy as it may sound, I would rather pay higher rates to a private lender and avoid the massive amount of paperwork associated with a bank loan. Therefore, investors like myself who can easily qualify for bank loans, would rather work with private lenders, which is a much more efficient method. Moreover, private lending is better suited for our high volume business model which can be under a time crunch to close on the properties we place under contract.

For example, this month alone, my company is under contract to purchase eight houses. Even the thought of dealing with the banks for the purchase of these homes is too much to bear. Private mortgage lending is also commonly referred to as 'Relationship Based Lending', because the relationship that a borrower has with their lender means something. The fact that my private lenders help me streamline my business, make quick decisions on deals, and close fast is extremely valuable to me. My private lenders understand my business model as well as the process that my deals go through after I sign the contract. They know my attorney and transaction closing coordinator will be working behind the scenes to make sure everything is prepared properly and taken care of prior to closing while also keeping them in the loop along the way. I am more than happy to pay my lender's a higher rate of return simply in exchange for the speed in which these transactions occur and to avoid the red tape of the banks.

By the way, in no way, shape, or form does this mean that we are shortchanging our lenders by providing less paperwork. Rather, we are not under the guidelines of the government like the banks are that add tons of needless paperwork, procedures, reviews, approvals, etc. before a loan gets approved. This is not the case working with private lenders. I often say that private lending is "a handshake agreement backed up by the proper paperwork". And in the processes that we've used with our lenders for hundreds of deals, we make sure they always have the proper documentation and security and we always close at a title company. In later chapters, I'll talk more about what documents you will want to require for any deal that you invest.

So yes, believe it or not, for investors like myself that have the ability to obtain bank financing, dealing with the tremendous amounts of paperwork and red tape that banks require simply make banks an unattractive option for running a successful, high-volume investing business. Trust me, I have some great relationships with my bankers and still use them for new construction developments and long-term rental financing, but using them for loans to buy the investment properties that we purchase on a month to month basis that are required to close fast, just does not make sense.

SOME INVESTORS DON'T LOOK GOOD ON PAPER

As I mentioned earlier, there are a lot of real estate investors that don't look great to banks based on their financials. Banks simply do not take all circumstances into consideration when processing their loan applications. For banks, it's all about how the borrower looks on paper and less about the deal or "the rest of the story". So while there are certainly some investors that simply can't qualify for bank loans because of poor financials, there are other real estate investors that are very strong financially, but the banks simply don't like a certain aspect of their financials for whatever reason.

One example of this is lack of W2 income. Many investors have left their previous W2 jobs to pursue real estate full-time. Banks typically want to see at least two years of W2 or business income. So even if the real estate investor has solid financials, a simple bank checklist requirement may eliminate them from qualifying for a loan. For a real estate investor like this, it doesn't make sense for them to waste their time applying for a bank loan.

The simple point is that banks view customers financials differently than private lenders. I've already shared the scenario of a self-employed real estate investor with a lack of W2 income to show the bank which causes many, if not most, traditional lenders to deny their application. The same is true for young adults who have not yet had the time to establish an acceptable credit score. Though these individuals may have the education, experience, and even the cash to show they know what they are doing when it comes to real estate investing, this doesn't come across on the paperwork the bank requires for a loan application, and therefore, it is not considered as part of the approval process.

LACK OF CASH AND MONEY DOWN

Let's face it, some investors just don't have the cash to put down that the banks require. A lack of cash can be due to poor financials, or a lack of cash reserves due to the volume of their business and the amount of deals under contract. Currently, our company has over 50 properties in our inventory. Typically, about 25% of our inventory are flip projects under renovation therefore, we are making loan payments, utilities, insurance, etc. each and every month. At the same time we are paying out, on average, over $150,000 in construction costs to renovate these properties. Because these properties are under renovation, they obviously are not producing income for us like our rental properties, the other 75% of our inventory. Needless to say, the real estate investing business is a very cash intensive business. The thought of putting down 10 - 20% to buy properties with multiple other projects going on can be a huge reason real estate investors avoid borrowing from the banks. Private lender options are available wherein there is not a requirement to put any money down on the deal. Therefore, the money down requirement limits the types of deals and the amount of deals real estate investors are able to do with bank loans, if not totally eliminating banks as an option.

PRIVATE LENDING TO THE RESCUE!

All of the previous circumstances create an opportunity for private mortgage lending, which makes financial sense for both the borrower and lender. On an annual basis, private mortgage lenders loan billions of dollars that other institutional lenders can't, or choose not to fund. Add to the mix the ever present uncertainty in the stock market, private mortgage investing is on the rise to say the least. It all comes down to this, real estate investors need money to purchase investment properties and the ability to close quickly. Private mortgage lenders want to invest in sound investments secured by real estate while at the same time earning above market rates of return. Let me say that again because the last two sentences really encapsulate what this book is all about:

Key Point 1: Investors need money to purchase investment properties and the ability to close quickly.

Key Point 2: Private mortgage lenders want to invest in sound investments secured by real estate while at the same time earning above market rates of return.

If real estate investors are not able to get a loan from a bank, or the bank will take too long to process their application, then they need to find other avenues to finance their deals. While they do have the option to work with a hard money lender, or an asset-based financier, this is very expensive for the real estate investor. This makes it hard for them to earn acceptable returns on their deals due to high interest rates and fees paid to the hard money lenders.

Essentially, the private mortgage lender fills the gap between banks and the hard money lenders or loan sharks, who are often overpriced and have some cumbersome processes to work through for investors. With private mortgage lending, instead of paying interest to a bank, borrowers can pay interest to their friends, family members, or others who have money to lend. Since the private mortgage lender benefits from making money with minimal risk, it creates an attractive win-win deal for both the borrower and the lender, and this simply isn't consistently possible with traditional loans or hard money lenders.

In my real estate coaching business, I work with people that are just getting started in real estate investing. Many of my students have a very successful track record and accolades from their work experience and have a background of financial success, and could easily qualify for bank loans. However, as they go through my training and learn about all of the different financing options they have, guess what is their number one method that they utilize to finance their deals? You guessed it, private money lenders! Private lending has become the preferred financing source for real estate investors.

CHAPTER TAKEAWAYS

Banks simply do not provide the lending options that real estate investors need in order to get access to the capital when they need it. Though banks can offer better interest rates, they have strict requirements and a longer timeline.

As you move forward in this book and your journey toward becoming a private mortgage lender, keep the following in mind:

- Not all investors are able to get approved for a bank loan, but this doesn't always mean they are not worthy borrowers
- With the right process and documentation in place, private mortgage lending can help you make money with minimal risk
- Private mortgage lending creates an ideal "win-win" situation for both the borrower and the lender
- There are billions of dollars invested every year in Private mortgage loans and demand is increasing significantly every year

There is a huge opportunity for private lenders in today's market to fill the gap between the banks and hard money lenders. Private lenders that take advantage of this investment strategy can truly take advantage of a huge opportunity that the banks are failing to capitalize on.

Chapter 3: Myths, Misconceptions and Pitfalls

"Successful investing is about managing risk, not avoiding it."

– Benjamin Graham

In this chapter, I'll talk about some of the fears, myths, and misconceptions that surround private mortgage lending and explain why they just aren't accurate when you are applying some of the proven fundamentals of lending that we will cover throughout this book. I'll also cover some of the common pitfalls that private mortgage lenders, especially those who are new to lending, often experience. This should help you get a better idea of what private mortgage lending entails while preparing you for the challenges that could hold you back from success.

I would say the first step towards becoming a successful private mortgage lender, is overcoming any fears and misguided ideas about what private mortgage lending is and how it works. Like most things, knowledge is your friend here, as a lack of understanding about private mortgage lending can ultimately lead to undesirable outcomes. As you start to increase your knowledge about the private mortgage lending opportunity, You will find that your fears and anxieties will disappear. More importantly, your chances of making mistakes will drastically be reduced and when you learn the right way to identify great deals and structure loans, you will be on your way to becoming a confident and experienced private mortgage lender.

COMMON FEARS ABOUT PRIVATE LENDING

As with any type of investment, there are a few common fears that hold people back from becoming private mortgage lenders. For the most part, you can overcome these fears by doing a little research and learning the right way to set up your deals so that you are minimizing risk and working to properly secure your investment.

One of the biggest fears new lenders have about private mortgage lending is whether their financial security will be affected, especially if something were to go wrong. First, let me say that a lender, whether private or traditional, is always taking a risk. No matter what type of investing you do, there will always be risk and a chance that something could go wrong. Private mortgage lending is no exception. Every lender needs to do their homework to figure out whether an investment is worthwhile before entering into any type of agreement.

With that being said, by no means should a private lender trust a borrower who claims to have an investment that is 100% safe or a loan that they can guarantee 100%. This is not plausible in the world of investing. You should always do your due diligence, no matter how much an investor ensures you there is little risk in their investment. Run the numbers yourself to see if the investment makes sense.

Though it may seem impossible to overcome this fear, with the right knowledge and time-tested advice, you can work to minimize your risk to better enjoy the benefits of private lending. In this book, I'm going to lay out a simple and proven process to help you secure your investment and make sure you are minimizing risks each step of the way and setting yourself up to profit even if a deal goes "bad".

Another common fear that prospective lenders have is they will not get back their capital. When done properly, private mortgage lenders require a mortgage that is clearly secured by the real estate. A secured mortgage will help protect the lender's interest. In fact, the term "mortgage" technically means security, not loan. Again, later in this book, I will provide everything you need to know about structuring your loans properly to minimize risks.

Some final fears that private lenders might have pertain to improper loan documentation or a borrower not having insurance for the property. These are valid concerns, but again, if you follow the proper procedures that are outlined in this book, it will not be an issue because these are 'checklist' items that you will not fund a deal until you have received these documents and had an opportunity to review and approve them. In later chapters, I will discuss how to safeguard your loans with the correct paperwork and insurance policies while also going into more detail about other procedures that will help you safely protect your invested capital.

PRIVATE MORTGAGE LENDING MYTHS BUSTED

As I mentioned in the beginning of the book, one of the biggest myths that prospective investors have about private mortgage lending is that it is only for professionals with years of experience. I cannot stress enough the myth that abounds in that statement. Anyone can learn to become a private mortgage lender. It requires some basic knowledge and some due diligence with each deal, but it is not something reserved for only experienced investors. Anyone who works to understand the proper process and is diligent about documentation can enjoy the benefits of private mortgage lending. As a matter of fact, after reading this book, you will likely know more than a majority of the private lenders currently in the marketplace. It is safe to say that you are on track to building a very strong base of knowledge to support a successful lending future!

On that same note, many people think they have to have millions in funds to get started as a private mortgage lender. When you look at the people who have actually become successful as private lenders, you'll find this just isn't the case. Though they have been able to build wealth over time, not every lender started with millions of dollars to invest. In fact, I worked with private mortgage lenders that started with less than $50,000 to invest. However, many of my lenders typically have around $100,000 to invest. Of course, some of them have much more, while others have less. I've even worked with a few private lenders with as little as $20,000. This provides great opportunities for potential lenders who want to get started with smaller amounts of capital to invest.

Another common myth that I absolutely love to debunk is that foreclosure is one of the worst things that can happen to a lender. A lot of novice lenders fear the thought of taking a property back from a borrower and having to foreclose. First off, depending on which state you live in, the foreclosure process can be relatively easy. Secondly, if you've structured your deal correctly and within the formula guidelines that we will discuss later, there is a very strong possibility that you as a lender, could come out much more profitable on the deal. As a matter of fact, multiple lenders that I work with have had to foreclose on properties in the past with other borrowers and in most every instance, they've come out ahead making substantially more money on the deal having to foreclose than they would have if the borrower had actually performed as intended!

While foreclosure isn't an ideal scenario and is not something you would ever want to deal with, be assured, when you perform the proper due diligence up front, the cards are stacked favorably in your behalf. This means that you stand to come away with a profitable return even if the "worst case" scenario of foreclosure is the result. I know it is counterintuitive, but many lenders have seen this firsthand. They thought a foreclosure could be the worst thing to happen with their investment. However, at the end of the day, rather than making a simple 7-10% return, they end up making a return in the 20-30% range and sometimes even more. This is when I get a call from them asking me to coach and teach them how to flip houses after they see how profitable it can be!

As we all know, everyone has to start somewhere, and everyone starts at some point with zero knowledge and zero experience. Even if you have never invested before, or you only have a small amount of capital to invest, with the right tools, knowledge, and resources, you can become a successful private mortgage lender. Don't get caught up in the fact that you are not as experienced as other investors. In time, you will learn what you need to know and be on your way to enjoying the benefits of making money with minimal risk. Just the fact that you are reading this book means that you are taking initiative to arm yourself with the knowledge and resources to become successful.

Look Out for These Pitfalls

Are there any pitfalls to be concerned about? Absolutely. There are some common pitfalls that you will need to contend with when becoming a private mortgage lender. By understanding these pitfalls, looking out for them, and working to avoid them, you can help minimize risk and lower your chances of losing out on a deal.

Investing in Something You Don't Understand

One of the fundamental rules of investing is you should never invest in something that you don't understand. One of the great things about becoming a private money lender to real estate investors is they specialize in single-family homes. Typically, single family home investing is a straightforward investment. For the most part most people understand how the investing process works While there may be a few aspects or technicalities that can cause some confusion, single-family homes overall are a fairly simple investment. Nevertheless, a common pitfall I see is when investors don't understand something and they fail to clarify with the title company, the borrower, or their attorney prior to moving forward.

This happens a lot in complex apartment deals and other types of commercial investments that private lenders make even though they don't really understand the numbers or the transaction itself. Confusion can also happen when private lenders are just starting out. The old adage, "there is no such thing as a stupid question" applies here. Simply put, if you don't understand something, just ask someone. And if you still don't understand, don't do the deal!

Avoid the following pitfall by doing some basic evaluation. Analyze the borrower, the deal, and any aspect of the deal that you don't understand or have a concern about. Before you enter into a deal with a borrower, get to know them and understand what their experience level is as well as how they run their business model. Ask for referrals and learn more about their previous deals, including how they have overcome any challenges in the past. Make sure that you understand what it is you are investing in so you can avoid this common pitfall.

INVESTING WITH SOMEONE WHO LACKS CHARACTER

Another major pitfall is investing with someone who lacks the character to still perform when they are faced with adversity in their business. Trust me, everyone experiences challenges. As a matter of fact, Nathan Long of Quest IRA, who will be joining me later in the book to discuss how to use your Self-Directed IRA to invest as a private mortgage lender, often says, "I don't like to lend to a real estate investor who says they've never lost money on a deal." His reasoning for this is if someone says they have never lost money on a deal, he feels they're either lying or they simply don't have enough experience as an investor, and I agree one hundred percent.

At some point in time, all veteran, full-time real estate investors will experience a loss. However, what is important is how they perform with their lenders during these times when deals go 'bad'. This is where true character is exposed. And just in case you're wondering, yes, I have had deals go bad and I've lost money on several deals. But guess what? I have always performed according to my loan agreements with my lenders. They have made the exact return that I agreed to according to the loan documents. As a matter of fact, many of my lenders never knew of some of the issues I suffered on these 'bad' deals because I continued to send their monthly interest payments like clockwork as well as their payoff of their loan as agreed upon, despite the challenges that I faced with the deal.

I understand that everyone has to start somewhere in this business, meaning every experienced real estate investor was a rookie at some point in time, including myself. I am incredibly thankful for those who trusted me and invested with me back in the beginning; and I'm proud to say that 11+ years later, I am still in the business. After completing hundreds of successful deals and a few bad ones, the thing I'm most proud of is I've kept a 100% track record of performance to my lenders even when I personally have taken losses.

To be able to say that I've successfully borrowed and paid back tens of millions of dollars to buy single-family homes while keeping a perfect track record with my lenders on every single one of my deals means a lot. Once again, this does not mean that I haven't lost money on any of my deals because like I said, I have. However, even though I have lost money on a few deals doesn't mean that my lenders lost money because my integrity and reputation means more to me than trying to get off the hook when a deal goes sideways. I want to stress this point because it is absolutely critical you find borrowers that are of high character and high integrity, because if they are lacking in this area, you are setting yourself up for an ugly situation when one of their real estate deals goes 'sideways'.

Not only is it highly critical that you find borrowers with strong character, but I would also suggest that you only invest with borrowers that are willing to sign a 'Personal Guarantee' document. My attorney prepares a personal guarantee document that I sign and provide to my lenders on every deal and I suggest you require the same from your borrowers. That way, even if their deal isn't working out as planned, they still perform according to the agreement laid out in the loan documents they signed with you and you have a personal guarantee that can provide some additional accountability to recoup any potential losses you may incur.

INVESTING WITH A NEW REAL ESTATE INVESTOR

Investing with a beginning real estate investor can certainly be a potential pitfall or risk that you may not want to venture into if you are also a new private lender. This does not mean that you should avoid working with new investors, but you want to feel confident they will be able to get the deal done.

If you choose to work with a new real estate investor and they have little to no experience, it is vital you make sure they have an experienced team behind them to support them through the process. For example, many of my lenders will lend to my coaching students, even if it's their first deal simply because they know I'm in the corner of my students who are fledgling real estate investors. So if a new investor has a strong team and mentor or coach, this can certainly be considered a credit to them.

Some private mortgage lenders will safeguard themselves when working with new real estate investors by requiring them to invest some of their own money in the deal, also known as having "skin in the game." This is not a hard and fast requirement, however, it can help you better determine how serious, confident and invested a borrower is. If a new real estate investor is willing to put their own money into the deal, this is a sign they are confident in their abilities, which can inspire confidence in a private lender.

If you are a new private money lender, the thought of working with a newbie investor may not be the best scenario, but as you start to become a more experienced lender, you may consider working with new investors simply because you can typically charge higher interest and get bigger returns. When I speak about private lending at networking events, I often like to use this phrase for a lender to determine the skill level of their borrowers, "You can often tell the experience of the investor by what they pay for their money". In other words, though there is more risk when working with new real estate investors, they will typically pay higher interest than someone who is more experienced.

For example, when I'm lending on deals to other real estate investors, I specifically target newer real estate investors to loan to simply because I can earn a higher rate of return and charge more points. I am also very comfortable with the deals that I'm loaning on and have the ability to thoroughly screen the borrowers to safeguard myself. In the event I need to foreclose and take a property back, I'm very comfortable with that scenario, but this is something you need to be comfortable with yourself before moving forward on any deal. The general pattern I have seen play out in the real world following this typical progression; less experienced lenders tend to loan to more experienced borrowers and conversely, more experienced lenders tend to make loans to less experienced borrowers.

NOT REQUIRING STANDARD DOCUMENTATION OR CLOSING AT A TITLE COMPANY

Something I would consider non-negotiable is to require your borrower to pay for and provide a Title Insurance Policy. This policy assures there are no other liens, mortgages, or interests that conflict with your interest as a private mortgage lender. In other words, you want to be sure your private money lien is in first lien position.

Most borrowers typically only purchase and provide what is called an Owner's Policy. This policy protects the borrower in the event some issue arises with the title. Some issues that arise occasionally are forgery, errors or omissions in previous deeds, mistakes/oversights when examining records, undisclosed heirs, etc. Basically what this policy does is act as insurance to protect the borrower/owner so that the title company will step in and provide legal defense and resources as needed to resolve the problem or compensate for any losses incurred.

Another type of title insurance is called a Lender's Title Policy, also called a "'Loan Policy". This is something that our company always provides and pays for our private lenders to further insure their interest as the lender. This policy protects the lender's interests should a problem with the title of the property surface. This policy does not protect the borrower, it only protects the lender. Fortunately, my lenders have never had to utilize this coverage, but it is worth the cost to me to provide my lenders peace of mind knowing this is yet another way their loan is secured. From what I've gathered from talking to others in the industry, this isn't a policy that most other real estate investors provide to their lenders, but my advice to you is to require it on every deal and to have your borrower pay for this policy as well.

After completing hundreds of deals, I will tell you that I've never had any major title issues. But certainly do your due diligence and be prepared and insured in the event something does occur.

WIRING OR SENDING MONEY DIRECTLY TO A BORROWER

A word of advice: Never wire or send money directly to an investor for a real estate purchase. I always have our lenders wire money to the title company so everything is documented on the settlement statements and legal docs are properly recorded in the properties respective county. Every one of our deals are always done "above board" and documented with paperwork from my attorneys. Closing is done at the title company or with my attorneys. Remember, while private lending essentially originates from a general discussion and a handshake agreement, it must always be followed up and carried out with the proper paperwork and procedures or you could be exposing yourself to many risks that could easily be avoided.

LENDING TO FRIENDS AND FAMILY MEMBERS

Many new private mortgage lenders ask me about whether or not they should lend to friends and family members. I have a simple answer to that. If it is a relationship that you would regret losing if something went wrong with the deal, then the answer is an easy no. Avoid the pitfalls of investing with someone you love and admire unless you are 100% confident of their ability to perform and 100% okay that if something were to go wrong, your relationship would be able to withstand that scenario.

Another way to tackle this issue is to ask yourself if you will be able to handle the potential friend or family member borrower in a complete businesslike manner even if the worst case scenario occurs? I know that some people are very even tempered, and do well handling their emotions in difficult situations, so this may not be a difficult task for them. However, I know that many others have a challenge withholding emotions, especially with friends and family members, so for that reason, this scenario would not likely make very much sense for the emotional types.

LENDING ON A DEAL WITHOUT ENOUGH EQUITY

When you lend on a deal without 'enough' equity you are not only falling into a potential pitfall, you are eliminating your 'saving grace' in the event other things go sideways. You must establish what your minimum amount of equity is for a deal so that you have room to breathe in the event something goes wrong. Equity in a deal is as essential as oxygen, It gives you time and space to breathe to navigate through the situation and still come out on top. As a matter of fact, when you follow the guidelines that we establish later in the chapter, 'How To Analyze A Deal', not only will you give yourself oxygen to breathe, you will have set yourself up to make a substantially higher return than just acting as the lender!

I understand for most lenders reading this, your intention is to never have to take back possession of a home you've loaned on. But t I feel it is best to put yourself in position to profit in the event an equity situation like this should ever occur. I've seen too many lenders loan to investors without the proper amount of equity. When things went wrong, the lenders unfortunately had to take back properties without adequate equity. I have also seen lenders who have required the correct amount of equity and the property had to be taken back, needless to say, they were smiling all the way to the bank!

Chapter Takeaways

While there are many myths, misconceptions and pitfalls that exist, as you increase your knowledge about the subject of private mortgage lending, your fear should begin to subside while your confidence increases. Don't let these typical fears that people have hold you back from reaping the rewards of this powerful investment opportunity. Rather, learn to eliminate or mitigate the risks and set yourself up for success.

In the end, you must remember that a private mortgage loan is an investment and there will always be associated risks with any investment. So as you go through this book, develop a strategy to avoid the pitfalls discussed in this chapter and begin to apply the proven lending fundamentals that have been shared that successful lenders employ.

Above all else, remember that learning how to become a private mortgage lender is well within your grasp, It is not restricted to the elite and experienced. Everything worth doing is also worth taking the time to learn how to do it correctly. By following the steps that I will lay out in the next few chapters, you will be well on your way to learning how to become a private mortgage lender while minimizing risks and avoiding potential pitfalls.

Be sure to visit the
Private Lender Playbook page
to access valuable tools & resources

www.PrivateLenderPlaybook.com

Chapter 4: Hard Money Lenders

"Everyone wants a piece of land. It's the only sure investment, it can never depreciate like a car or a washing machine."

– Russel Sage

Earlier in the book we talked about why there is a need for private lending and how private mortgage lenders help fill in the gap left by the banks and the hard money lenders for real estate investors needing a loan. But who exactly are hard money lenders and what do they do and where do they fit into the mix? We haven't discussed hard money lenders in detail yet, but if you want to become a proficient private mortgage lender, I think it's important to understand the industry and other options that real estate investors have for getting the funds they need for their deals. I believe that as you begin to better understand the industry, you will be able to recognize the value of what you have to offer as a private lender.

In this chapter, I'll explain what hard money is and answer some common questions people often ask about hard money lending. I'll also discuss in additional details how private money is helping to fill the gaps between banks and hard money loans and why now is an incredible time to begin investing as a private mortgage lender.

HARD MONEY EXPLAINED

All loans, no matter what type, have one thing in common. There has to be some reasonable expectation that the borrower will eventually be able to repay the loan. As we discussed in an earlier chapter, traditional banks use a lengthy application process to determine a borrower's ability to repay. This often requires a great credit score, favorable debt to income ratio, and other financial documents serving as proof of their financial portfolio position. But HMLs take a slightly different approach.

Hard money lenders, for the context of this book, are basically small companies, groups, or funds that lend money to real estate investors, called hard money, based on the investment property's value. They are often times called 'Asset Based Lenders', because they value the asset more so than the borrower. For rehab investment projects, they consider the future value of the property based on the repairs that are going to be done much more so than the credit worthiness of the borrower. Because HMLs are asset-based lenders, it simply means they are more concerned about the asset than, they are the borrower, but that being said, HMLs do consider the borrower's financials and experience into their lending decision equation. But once again, they place more emphasis and focus of their analysis into the property and the financial projections of the deal more so than how the borrower looks on paper.

Overall, hard money lenders are most concerned about the collateral that is securing the loan. If something were to go wrong with the deal or borrower and the real estate investor could not pay the loan, hard money lenders plan to get their investment back by taking the collateral and selling it. They are very thorough in their due diligence to make sure they will be able to not only take the property back with equity, but also provide themselves enough equity to easily sell the property to recoup their invested capital.

Hard money loans are typically short-term loans, lasting between six months to one year. Percentage-wise, these loans cost much more than an average bank mortgage with typical hard money loan interest rates falling in the 12 - 18% range. In addition, they also have high origination fees. A typical bank will charge .5 to 1% of the overall loan amount as an origination fee or processing fee, while hard money lenders will typically charge between 2 and 4% in origination fees. You don't have to be a math whiz to see how profitable this can be for the lenders, and costly for an investor. For example, if an investor were to borrow $200,000 from a hard money lender that was charging 4 points to provide the loan, the real estate investor is shelling out $8,000 up front just to get started. There are still additional fees and closing costs on top of that and the monthly interest payments are due typically thirty days after the loan begins!

So why did hard money loans come into existence?

In the past, real estate investors typically turned to banks when they needed a loan. However, as I discussed previously, most banks have a long list of strict requirements and a timeline that is not conducive to the average investment real estate deal. Given these circumstances, those in the industry quickly realized there was a need for an alternative lending source.

It became obvious to those who had the necessary funds available that they could better serve real estate investors than the banks could. Not to mention, there was a huge opportunity for them to make incredible rates of return in the process. Hard money companies began to surface, and they quickly became a critical component to the real estate investment industry. In fact, many hard money lenders are making it possible for the average real estate investor to get started in the real estate investing business.

Truth be told, hard money lenders provide a very useful service to the real estate industry. As a real estate coach and speaker, I often recommend that beginning real estate investors start with hard money to get their feet wet and learn the ropes of the industry. Hard money lenders are often great for new investors who are just getting started because they act as a safeguard to provide some guidance on their deals. HMLs are in the business of analyzing deals and deciding whether they are viable, making them a great resource for new investors who are just learning what makes a great deal. I've always said having a HML look over the shoulder of a rookie real estate investor to analyze their deal is excellent real-world education for new real estate investors just coming into the market.

I love to share this story when I'm speaking, about one of the HMLs I was working with during my first year in real estate and they would not fund one of my deals. First, let me go back in time to give you some insight. My first year in real estate I was exclusively working with HMLs to fund my initial, front side acquisition of properties. Meaning every time I placed a new property under contract, they would loan me the money to purchase and renovate the house, then I would go to my mortgage broker to refinance their loan into a long-term financing from the bank.

The hard money lender would receive their payoff at closing and I would have long-term financing from the banks with 6-7% interest loans with fully amortized loans on my now completely renovated properties. I did this successfully ten times my first year in real estate, but on one of my deals, my hard money lender, said "No". He would not approve me for the loan on that particular deal! At that time, I was around my fifth investment deal in my young career, so perhaps my ego was beginning to think I was the next real estate tycoon, because I recall taking offense to the rejection. But in hindsight after a little time to think about it, my HML friend had really done an incredible favor. He provided some real world education on several construction items that I had completely missed and filled me in on some other information in an the area that I was not privy to. I gladly thanked him for the real world education and gladly walked away from the deal. This is why I like new real estate investors who aren't working with a coach or mentor to strongly consider beginning with hard money lenders as their financing source before they progress to private money loans.

WHO TYPICALLY BORROWS FROM HMLS AND WHY?

In short, the people who want to borrow from private mortgage lenders are the same people who borrow from hard money lenders – real estate investors, developers, and house flippers who need money to fund their deals and don't have a more viable, less expensive financing option. Though each hard money lender may have slightly different rates, terms and guidelines, these types of loans allow real estate investors to cut through the red tape and easily access the money they need to move quickly on deals, however, it comes with terms that are, forgive the pun, 'hard' to swallow.

Many investors turn to hard money because quite frankly, it may be the only option they have if they do not have a private mortgage lender they can borrow from. And the hard money loan, quite frankly, accomplishes their goal. The borrower can typically borrow close to 100% of the purchase price from the HML and get the funding they need within 7 to 14 days, as opposed to a bank loan which can take an obnoxious amount of time, that is, if they can even qualify for it. And once an investor has built a relationship with a HML, they may even be able to get funds within just a few days, allowing them to act faster on attractive deals that must close quickly. Like we've discussed before, this ability to close quickly is many times the deciding factor if they can keep or lose the deal.

Borrowing from a hard money lender for most, if not all real estate investors, really comes down to a business conversation and turning to the numbers. For me, when I was using HMLs for financing, if the numbers of the deal still worked with their rates and fees, then I would do the deal. If not, then I would walk away. The same thing is true to this day. This is why hard money continues to exist as an industry because rather than missing out on a deal with a potentially big payoff, real estate investors will opt for using a costly and expensive hard money loan to get the funds they need when they need it. The hard money allows the investor access to the deal rather than walking away and not making a dime. Therefore, for many real estate investors, HMLs are their only hope.

Whether real estate investors use HMLs for quick turn short-term flips or for financing the initial purchase of properties they are going to rehab and refinance to keep as a rental, either way, this has been the 'industry standard' financing option for most investors for a very long time. While hard money loans can be a great resource for new investors, they are not cost effective and financially viable to real estate investors over the long-term. Most real estate investors, particularly those who are new to the industry, need to work to build their credit and their business, and hard money offers them a way to get started in the beginning and gain very valuable experience. I've seen most investors make the same progression I made, which was from more expensive/costly financing (HMLs) in the beginning to more favorable financing terms and relationships with Private Money Lenders as they build their experience and investment portfolio.

How Private Money is Filling the Gap Between Banks and Hard Money

I think you're probably beginning to see how HMLs can be a necessary channel for real estate investors that have no other way to get the funds they need. Trust me, I relied exclusively on hard money to finance my deals in the beginning of my investing career so I know all about it. If it were not for hard money lenders, I don't know what I would have done as a beginning investor. I'm also glad to say that I made a lot of money in the real estate business because of my relationships with the hard money lenders that I used in the beginning, I know first-hand that HMLs play an important role in the industry. But I soon realized that I was also at the same time, making my HMLs a lot of money as well, I would even say, too much!

So for obvious reasons, hard money loans are not the most ideal source of financing for experienced investors. Much like training wheels for a child who is just learning how to ride a bike, hard money loans are great for real estate investors who are just getting started. But at some point, real estate investors that are going to progress to the next level, have to take the training wheels off as they gain more experience in order to take their business to a more stable and sustainable business model. Similarly, for passive lenders and stock market investors, possibly like yourself, mutual funds and cd's may be the training wheels for most, but private mortgage lending is definitely for those investors that are ready to take the training wheels off!

Though hard money lenders allow investors to borrow money quickly and without all the strict requirements of a bank, they are also extremely expensive like I've mentioned. If investors want to make a profit on a property they buy with a hard money loan, they have to buy the property at an extremely discounted rate and everything must go according to plan with the deal, leaving little room for error. Typically, real estate investors will have to pay double-digit interest rates on hard money loans as well as high origination fees, which can sometimes make it hard for them to come out on the other end with a profit on the balance sheet.

Overall, private money lenders help fill in the gap between banks and hard money lenders through a combination of offering both favorable speed and pricing. Many banks don't want to offer short-term loans, and, if approved, it takes excessive amounts of time for borrowers to get access to the capital that they need. Private mortgage lenders offer shorter terms with quicker access to capital for real estate investors. In addition, private money lenders are more likely to make loans that the average bank would typically pass on. But this does not mean they are bad investments simply because the banks are not funding them, rather, its the red tape that prevents them the flexibility to take advantage of investment opportunities that are ideal for private money lenders.

Additionally, while hard money can offer quick access to capital, it also costs the investor a significant amount to obtain. Private mortgage lenders are able to provide better rates than hard money lenders, making it possible for both the lender and the real estate investor to come out on top. Many investors also prefer to work with private mortgage lenders over HMLs because they enjoy working directly with regular folks rather than working with a company or through a middle man. And trust me, this may not seem like a big deal, but it really is. One of my greatest joys in my business is helping my private lenders grow their investment accounts and net worth while at the same time helping to grow my business. It is an incredibly symbiotic relationship and I'm proud to call them my friends.

Why Now is a Good Time to Get Started with Private Mortgages for Real Estate

Here's the deal, in recent years, hard money lenders have gotten greedy and have begun to 'monopolize' the space, so to speak. They know the banks processes and guidelines simply don't work for real estate investors, and they have taken advantage of this fact by charging extremely high interest rates and fees that make it more and more difficult for investors to be profitable with their deals as well as create a sustainable business model. This greediness has created a tremendous opportunity for private mortgage lenders who want to offer an alternative financing option for trustworthy and experienced real estate investors. Real estate investors turn to private money lenders when they need fast access to capital without the high fees and other obstacles of hard money. When done correctly, private mortgage lending allows you to mitigate risk while simultaneously building wealth and establishing a consistent stream of income.

Of course, this is not a path that everyone can walk. First, you must ask yourself if you can afford to do so. Having a little extra money in the bank does not mean that you should throw it at the first real estate investor that comes your way. In fact, if this is your first instinct, that's a pretty good sign that you are not yet ready to become a private mortgage lender.

It is vital that you take the time to understand the industry risks as a whole. If you're not willing to do this, then private lending is not a good fit. However, if you are equipped to mitigate potential risks and take advantage of the opportunities that present themselves, then you may want to further consider the benefits of becoming a private mortgage lender.

CHAPTER TAKEAWAYS

While hard money lenders provide a viable option for real estate investors to finance their deals, they are in no way, shape or form the most ideal option. Simply put, hard money lending rates and terms have gotten too expensive for most real estate investors to run a sustainable investing business.

Private lending has stepped up to fill the gap between banks and hard money lenders by offering a combination of speed and reasonable rates. This has created an incredible opportunity for private lenders that are educated, equipped and have the means and the desire to succeed in this investment opportunity.

Chapter 5: How to Pick Your Ideal Investment

"Real estate is about the safest investment in the world."

– Franklin D. Roosevelt

The question that I probably get asked most often from new and aspiring private mortgage lenders is – How do you know if something is a good investment? This is a bit of a loaded question, and it requires some unpacking to answer properly. Every private lender is different in terms of their ability to loan, their risk tolerance and desired outcomes. Though there is no one-size-fits-all answer to the question of how to pick your ideal investment, there are a few basic factors that you will need to consider before you get started.

In this chapter, I'm going to provide you some other things to consider when choosing an investment opportunity. I'll also talk about what you need to determine before you even start looking for opportunities to invest, and I'll dive deeper into the difference between short and long-term investments and what each one means to you as a private mortgage lender.

CLARIFY WHAT TYPE OF INVESTMENT YOU'RE LOOKING FOR

First, I want to re-emphasize a common rule of investing – never invest in anything that you don't understand. This is something mentioned earlier in the book, but it is a very important rule to follow as a private mortgage lender and worth repeating! When considering any type of investment, make sure that you do your homework and understand what you are investing in!

It helps to start by clarifying which types of investments work best for your needs, interests, and circumstances. As you begin looking into new opportunities to invest with real estate investors, it's important to go through this list of items to ensure that you are clear on what type of investment you are looking for.

SHORT VS. LONG-TERM FINANCIAL GOALS

Before you lend even a dime to an investor, you need to clearly define your short and long-term financial goals. Then, consider where investing fits into this goal. Short-term goals are typically those that can be accomplished within a year or two. Maybe you want to make a certain dollar amount from your investments so that you can go on vacation or help pay for your child's impending college education. Whatever your goals are, be sure to outline these financial targets so that you can align your investing strategy as needed to help get you closer to achieving them.

Though it's great to think about how investing can impact your near future, it's also vital that you consider where you want to be long-term as this will have an impact on your strategy and affect the types of deals that you invest in as a private mortgage lender. Most likely, your money needs to keep working for you far into the future, even if you are already retired. The best way to get a good understanding of where you want and need to be financially in the future is to do the work now to project your long-term cash flow.

You will need to find balance between your short-term and long-term priorities in order to align your investment strategy with these goals. For instance, if you want higher returns in the short-term, you may be faced with taking on more high risk deals that are typically flip properties with less experienced investors. But if your financial goals don't require high risk deals, or you simply are not a person with high risk tolerance, then you may want to adjust your investments to more long-term, low risk deals. Typically, these deals are found with more established real estate investors who are likely investing in rental properties, or longer term, more passive investments. We'll talk about both options in further detail as we progress.

RETURN REQUIREMENTS

What kind of return do you need from your portfolio? The answer to this question will tell you how conservative or aggressive your investment strategy needs to be as well as what types of deals to take on. If you're looking for higher returns, you will need a more aggressive investment strategy that might require you to take on riskier deals as previously mentioned. However, if you're looking for more moderate returns to build long-term wealth, then you can afford to adopt a more conservative strategy with less risk.

Risk Tolerance

How far are you willing to go to get the return you want? If you want higher returns, you'll have to take on more risk. However, not everyone has a high-risk tolerance. There are many factors that can impact your ability to tolerate risk in investments. Here are just a few that you may want to consider when determining your risk tolerance:

Age

Typically, the younger you are, the more risk you are able to tolerate. If things don't end up in your favor, you have more time to recover, and it's generally easier to bounce back. However, if you are older and living on a limited income in retirement, you may not be able to tolerate as much risk.

Annual Income

If you are looking to use the returns from your investments for normal living expenses, you will also want to consider if your annual income will stay the same, grow, or decrease in the future. If you do not anticipate that your income will continue to grow, you may not want to take on as much risk.

Expenses

Aspiring private mortgage lenders also need to consider which major expenditures they are paying for or anticipate paying for in the future. For instance, if you plan to pay for your child's education, and they are still young, you may be able to tolerate more risk when it comes to investing in the short-term.

It is vital that you are honest with yourself when it comes to your risk tolerance. If you invest aggressively as if you can take on all the risk in the world and some of your deals go 'south', you might find yourself in an unfavorable position, to put it lightly. Even though riskier deals and less experienced investors can often provide higher returns, you need to carefully consider whether or not you can assume the risks the deal might entail.

On that same note, be careful not to invest more than you have or over extend yourself. Investing can be exciting, but it's important to consider the realities of your circumstances before deploying your hard earned capital. I've said it before, and I'll say it again, every investment is a risk. That's why it is vital that you consider this risk before investing in any deal.

NON-NEGOTIABLES

In addition to considering the above factors, you will also want to create and adhere to a list of non-negotiables. These are things that you are not willing to do, no matter the circumstances and no matter the potential rate of return. For example, I would hope that it would not be negotiable for you to entertain any type of investment that violates your personal, ethical, or moral standards. Add those to the list of non-negotiables, and stick to your guns, no matter how much someone might try to convince you otherwise. At the end of the day, no matter how attractive an investment might seem, you need to be able to sleep at night knowing you remained steadfast in your principles and beliefs.

Another common non-negotiable for many private mortgage lenders is refraining from lending to friends or family members. I mentioned this earlier, but it's worth touching on again. My advice is to avoid lending to friends or family, unless you are 100% confident in their abilities as a real estate investor and 100% certain that your relationship could withstand the negative consequences of a bad deal. Again, if you decide you do not want to lend to friends or family, make sure that you stick to this non-negotiable, no matter how many times they may ask or how good the deal may seem. At the end of the day, your relationship is not worth what might happen if the deal goes south.

STICK TO THE INVESTMENT OPPORTUNITIES SUITED FOR YOU

There are a lot of different investment opportunities in the real estate market, but the focus of this book is on residential real estate, mostly because this is the easiest path for new private lenders to understand and master. In getting to know the potential investment opportunities in residential real estate, you will need to think about each type of investment and how it fits into your overall financial goals and other factors that impact your investment strategy.

Below, I'm going to breakdown the two main types of investments in the residential real estate arena – fix and flip properties, which tend to be short-term investments, and rental properties, which are typically long-term investments. Both types of investments are ideal for private mortgage lenders who want to grow their wealth with minimal risk. However, each has its own advantages, based on your overall financial goals and risk tolerance, which I will explain below.

FIX AND FLIP DEALS (SHORT-TERM INVESTMENTS)

When it comes to private mortgage lending, short-term investments are often made to lend on fix and flip deals that the real estate investor plans to purchase, renovate and sell. The life cycle of these types of deals are typically in the four to seven month range, but the loans are typically structured for a six-month to one-year term. These loans are usually interest only loans wherein the borrower only pays the interest on the mortgage paying monthly payments for a fixed term that has been agreed upon. Fix and flip loans are rarely amortized, but I have seen a few on occasion. While a lot of fix and flip deals are structured with fairly similar and standard terms, they can all have their own intricacies depending on the parameters and the game plan for each investor, lender and deal.

For instance, let's say that you lend $100,000 to an investor who buys a property for $75,000 and they plan to spend $25,000 in renovations and you've agreed to loan this money out at 10% interest with interest only payments due every month. The borrower has also provided a Comparative Market Analysis (CMA) showing the property will be worth approximately $135,000 after the repairs are complete. The borrower will begin to renovate the property and also pay you the interest for the agreed upon term as outlined in the promissory note, which would equate to $833.33 per month, for your invested amount of $100,000. These monthly interest payments typically begin 30 days after the purchase of the property was initially made. After completing the renovations to the property, the borrower will then list the property for sale with a realtor to sell for $135,000. After the property is listed, the borrower will hopefully receive an acceptable offer soon, but in the meantime, they will continue to make their monthly loan payments $833.33 to you each and every month.

After the real estate investor receives and agrees to an acceptable offer from a prospective buyer and has a closing scheduled to sell the property, you will be contacted by the title company to submit your payoff for the total amount of money that is due to you based on the loan. After you submit your payoff, with the exception of possibly a few emails or phone calls, you simply await until the closing occurs and make sure the title company has your correct bank wiring instructions so that you receive your payoff as soon as the sale and funding of the property is complete. After all closing documents are signed, you will receive your initial capital investment of $100,000 back, and any unpaid interest.

I used 10% interest in the previous example, but it's not unreasonable for fix and flip investors to pay 12 - 14% and sometimes even higher. Just remember what I mentioned earlier in the book, that you can tell the experience of the borrower by what they pay for their money. So while private lenders can potentially earn higher interest with fix and flip deals, these short-term investments are generally considered to have some additional risks because of the construction phase involved in flipping or rehabbing a property. Therefore, if you are considering a short-term fix and flip deal, it is beneficial to invest with real estate investors who have a solid track record of successful flip or rehab projects. If the investor is new to the industry, you may want to make sure they have a solid game plan and capability to complete a successful deal. It's also important to look at their previous business or professional experience. Make sure they have a solid team behind them, including a coach or mentor who will help guide them through the process. I've helped many of my students, starting with no experience, to successfully complete 5-10 successful flip deals in their first year of investing by following our proven process to find, fix and flip properties. I have also seen a countless number of real estate rookies come into the market and make some tragic investing mistakes.

Another downside to short-term loans is that you will have to regularly find new deals and real estate investors as your capital will be returned to you more frequently. With enough time and persistence, you will be able to find enough of the right kind of deals to meet your investment goals. However, if the idea of continuously looking for new deals and screening new real estate investors is something you do not have the time or desire to do, you may be more inclined to look at a long-term investment strategy and opportunities in that arena to keep your money actively working in the market for long stretches at a time.

RENTAL PROPERTIES
(LONG-TERM INVESTMENTS)

Long-term investments for private mortgage lenders typically come in the form of rental properties. Simply put, a real estate investor will purchase a property and hold it for the long-term as a positive cash producing asset. Rather than selling it, the real estate investor will rent the property out for many years to come. Some of these loan types may be for an existing property that is already renovated and leased out, but many start as a distressed property that requires a construction rehab in order to get the property to 'rent ready' status after the repairs are complete.

The loan terms on these types of investments can vary anywhere from one to five years. I have even seen them go for as long as 30 years, much like the banks, but this is a very rare instance and not advisable. And like the banks, these long-term rental loans are typically amortized, though not always, meaning the borrower pays back the loan through scheduled periodic payments consisting of both principal and interest.

Let's look at a Rental property loan example using the same loan amount numbers as the Flip investment example we used previously. So for instance, in this rental property case study, you also lend $100,000 to a landlord investor who is looking to buy a rental property for $75,000 and they plan to spend $25,000 in renovations, but this time you've agreed to loan at 7% interest, once again with interest only payments due every month. The borrower will begin to renovate the property and also pay you the interest for the agreed upon term as outlined in the promissory note. These payments would equate to $583.33 per month, for your invested amount of $100,000. Typically, monthly interest payments will begin 30 days after the purchase of the property or whatever date that is specified in the loan documents. After completing the renovations to the property, the borrower will then market the property for lease to a potential renter. Generally, 1% of the value of the home is a good rule of thumb. Therefore it will likely rent for approximately $1,350 per month. After the property is leased, the borrower will manage the asset, or higher a property management company to do so. Either way, you should continue to receive their monthly loan payments of $583.33 until the home is either sold or refinanced.

In a scenario like this, typically the real estate investor will refinance the loan with a bank at some point in time, but not always. Many times, real estate investors and lenders work out agreeable long-term loan structures that work for both sides. You see, some landlord investors aren't trying to pay the property off with an amortized loan, but rather they are seeking to cash-flow for 3-5 years and then sell the property to capture their equity and any appreciation that has occurred. So in an instance like this, an interest only loan for 3 - 5 years may work great for both sides. Another thing to note is that if you are not comfortable agreeing to a 3 - 5 year loan term, you can instruct your attorney to add an extension clause that the loan must receive your approval on an annual basis to be extended from year to year. This of course would be something you would also need to discuss and have your borrower agree to beforehand.

One benefit to long-term loans is they allow investors to avoid the hassle of continuously looking for places to invest their money. This allows private lenders to focus on what they find most important in life while their money is working for them behind the scenes. Though investors are willing to accept less interest on long-term loans as opposed to short-term loans, in many instances long-term investors end up coming out ahead due to the fact their capital is continuously working. Have you ever read the 'Tortoise and the Hare'? Yep, the same rule applies here.

TORTOISE AND THE HARE COMPARISON

Let's look at the tortoise and the hare conversation a bit more in depth with a 1-year snapshot for each investment option using the same investment example numbers as before. The average fix and flip deal lasts approximately 6 months, give or take. So let's say you decided to loan $100,000 on the fix and flip deal with monthly interest payments of $833.33 and the complete deal cycle from start to finish, lasted exactly six months. Your total return would be $4,999.98, net cash received. This is also assuming there were no origination points charged when the loan was issued. If you were unable to find another borrower to invest your capital with for the rest of the year, this $4,999.98 would be your total return, that would equate to a 5% net return on your money.

Conversely, let's say instead you decided to lend to the landlord investor for the loan amount of $100,000 for 7% interest. Because this is a rental property deal with a 3 - 5 year term, this loan was active and invested for the entire year earning $583.33 in interest per month. Your total return would be $6,999.96, net cash received. This is almost $2,000 more than the flip and flip strategy. This is just a basic example and something to consider as you work to define your ideal investment strategy and game-plan.

LIQUIDITY

Liquidity really comes down to your ability to generate the asset into cash. An example of highly liquid investments would be savings accounts and money market accounts. Of course, the more liquid an asset is, the safer it is generally considered to be, simply because of the speed and ease the ability the investor has to get their money out of the investment. Private mortgage lending is not considered a highly liquid investment because it certainly takes time to find an end buyer in the event you needed someone to purchase your note, or in the event you had to foreclose and sale the property because of borrower default, death, etc. This process could be a matter of days or months, depending on the type of property, the market and other variables.

So liquidity is another important consideration when considering your investment strategy. Before you loan money to a real estate investor, you need to consider the availability of your liquid assets. It's important that you are able to meet your personal short-term financial obligations without access to the money that you plan to invest in the deal. If you think that you will need this money that you're expecting to invest before the loan matures, then you should reconsider becoming a private lender at that time.

Even though most private loans pay off in the end as planned, as with any investment, there is always the possibility that it may not pay off as expected. If you want to be a successful private mortgage lender, it is imperative that you make sure you do not need access to the loan funds before the loan maturity date. That way, if something goes wrong with the deal, you will have time to wait for the appropriate payoff and will not put yourself in a tight spot financially if the deal doesn't pay off as you expected.

In the event that a private mortgage lender needs their invested capital returned before the loan maturity date, they do have the option of trying to sell the loan using an online loan exchange. They can also offer to sell the loan to another private mortgage lender through a loan broker. However, it's important to consider that these loans are typically sold at a discount, so the lender will still be taking a cut on the amount of capital they receive thus drastically slashing their rate of return, and possibly taking a loss. It should also be noted this type of transaction is very rare in the world of short-term private lending and not an ideal situation for you to be in.

CHAPTER TAKEAWAYS

Before you start looking for investment opportunities, you need to consider what types of investments are ideal for your unique personal circumstances. Take time to carefully consider your short-term and long-term financial goals, return requirements, risk tolerance, liquidity and non-negotiables before you look for opportunities. Additionally, you will need to take a look and weigh the pros and cons of short- and long-term loans before looking for borrowers.

Chapter 6: Analyzing the Borrower

> *"As I grow older, I pay less attention to what men say. I just watch what they do."*
>
> *– Andrew Carnegie*

Before we dive deeper into how the process of private lending works, let's first discuss some ways to analyze a potential borrower. In the previous chapter we discussed the different types of residential real estate investments that private lenders can be a part of – mainly, fix and flip, and rental properties. Once you recognize which type of real estate investment works best for your financial goals and investment strategy, then it is time to find the right borrowers for the type of deals you are looking for to invest.

In this chapter, I'll go more into detail about what you need to look for in the ideal borrower. Though it is vital to research your borrowers and do your due diligence on each deal, as a new private lender it is especially important that you follow the proper steps to ensure that a potential borrower is the right fit to help you achieve your investing goals.

EXPERIENCE

The first thing that you'll want to consider when looking at potential borrowers is their experience. Consider how long they have been working in the industry and look at their history of deals. Make sure they not only have experience as a real estate investor but also have experience investing in the types of properties they are purchasing. For instance, if they want to borrow on a fix and flip deal, you'll want to make sure they have a history of successful rehabs. If they don't have experience rehabbing homes, then you need to make sure the borrower has a well thought out plan and a proficient team in place to successfully navigate through all the potential twists and turns of that type of investment deal.

As I have said before, there is no hard and fast rule when deciding to invest with new real estate investors that have very little experience. There are plenty of new investors out there who have the knowledge and drive to become successful. However, as a new private mortgage lender, you need to be particularly selective in the beginning. Recognize the potential risks when working with new investors. If you are unable to tolerate this risk or you have any doubt in your mind that the investor will be able to successfully complete the deal, you may want to pass on the deal that time around and work with someone who has more experience. Once you gain experience as a private lender, you can benefit from working with new investors as they are more likely to pay higher interest rates for your money.

REFERENCES

Checking references is an important part of analyzing a borrower. Before you make any major investment, may I suggest you do your research into any company or individual that you are considering investing with and take the time to read any reviews and comments about them. There is no better way to determine how well a product works or how great a service is than by finding out more about the company and hearing from those who have had experience using the product or service first-hand from previous referrals.

The same is true of borrowers. As a private lender, checking a borrower's references can help you gain insight into their business practices, principles, and character. Most importantly, it is also one of the best ways to help you better determine if they will be able to repay the loan over time.

Unfortunately, there is no Yelp for real estate investors. However, there are a number of ways that you can determine whether a borrower is able to perform on a deal. The first is to ask for references from private lenders that have previously worked with the borrower. These lenders may be able to share some valuable insight as to what it was like to work with the borrower and whether there were any issues or concerns along the way. If that lender has worked with the borrower on multiple deals, this is a good sign that the real estate investor has gained their trust.

Though private lender references can go a long way in helping you analyze a borrower, they should not be the only type of reference you should use. You can look for other business accolades that show a borrower is serious about their work.

For example, my company, Invest Home Pro, has an A+ rating with the Better Business Bureau (BBB). We've been in business for over 10 years in the real estate investment industry, and my company has even appeared on the Inc. 5000 List of America's Fastest-Growing Private Companies. In addition, we have borrowed, and more importantly paid back, tens of millions of dollars to private lenders. We have never failed to perform on a single loan. In other words, we have a 100% success rate when it comes to performing for our lenders. These accomplishments say a lot about our experience and work ethic and provide proof of our ability to repay loans without any issues. This is the type of thing that you will want to look for when checking references for your potential borrowers. Not that your potential borrowers will have as many distinguished accomplishments, but a long-term track record, perhaps a positive standing with the BBB and a few other 'skins on the wall' can certainly help tilt the scales in their favor.

BUSINESS MODEL

As a private lender, you need to find out what your borrower's business model looks like. Whether you decide to have a conversation with them, look at their website, or even review their formal business plan, it's important to know what their investing business model is so that you can determine if this fits with your own short- and long-term investment plans, risk tolerance, and financial goals.

There are multiple avenues that a real estate investor might choose, and you will want to know upfront so that you are aware of any risks or potential issues that the investor could run into. For instance, if the borrower typically invests in single-family homes or rehab projects, this is typically riskier than rental properties. There are also many other types of properties that the borrower might specialize in, including multi-family homes, commercial properties, tax liens, etc. You will want to make sure that you are investing with someone that has a clear and focused business model before you agree to investing in one of their deals.

When exploring a potential borrower's business model, in addition to considering which types of properties they invest in, also focus on the property price points they typically invest in. It is also helpful to learn more about their short and long term investing goals as this can also impact their business model.

Borrower Credit

Most private money loans are based more on the asset or collateral. However, the best loans will give equal weight to the borrower's credit track record and capacity to repay when the loan matures or when a balloon payment becomes due. As I've mentioned before, just because a borrower doesn't have an excellent credit score or a long history of credit in general, this doesn't mean that you should completely disregard them. But a real estate investor's credit history can tell you a lot about what type of borrower they are. In addition, if you are just getting started as a private money lender, you will want to be a little more selective when it comes to a borrower's credit history.

Surprisingly, my private lenders have never asked for my credit score over the years. Though many private lenders don't want to see a credit score, I do encourage lenders to ask for a credit report. Even though this may not be the deciding factor in whether you lend to the potential borrower, it does show insight into the investor and is another valuable metric in helping you make a final decision when looking at all the other factors combined.

CAPACITY

In addition to looking at the borrower's credit, you will also want to consider the borrowers capacity, meaning the capacity to repay the loan. Their ability to repay the loan is one of the most important things to consider when accessing a borrower's creditworthiness. To determine the capacity, you'll want to look at:

- How much cash flow the business generates
- The borrower's payment history and track record of repayment
- How much debt the borrower has and what they can afford to repay
- Financial ratios such as debt to equity, debt to asset, and operating cash flow

COLLATERAL

The borrower's cash flow will be the main way that they repay the loan. However, collateral provides borrowers with a secondary source of repayment. The collateral is made up of the assets the borrower provides to you as a lender to secure the loan. In other words, the property. In the event that the borrower fails to repay, you as the lender will be able to seize the property as payment. This requires you to have the right paperwork in place and make sure the property has an acceptable amount of equity, but these are topics we will touch on in later chapters.

CAPITAL

The capital is the money the investor has personally invested in the deal. This money is at risk if the deal fails. Many private lenders are more likely to lend money to borrowers that have some of their own money into the deal, especially if the borrower is new to the industry. Having some of their own money in the deal shows the borrower has confidence in their abilities and they will do whatever it takes to make sure they don't default on the loan. Though it is not necessary for a borrower to put their own money into the deal, statistically speaking, it's a good sign they will perform dutifully.

CONDITIONS

The conditions of a loan refer to the overall economic climate in the borrower's industry and the broader economy. Here are some things you will want to consider when looking at the conditions:

- Current business climate
- Trends in the real estate investment industry
- Short- and long-term growth potential
- Economic or political issues that could negatively impact growth

CHARACTER

What is the general impression of the borrower? Though there are many objective factors that you will look at to determine whether it's the right borrower, you will also want to get a general impression of the borrower's character. To state the obvious, you only want to work with borrowers that are trustworthy. People that you know will do what it takes to perform on a deal. To get a better understanding of a real estate investor's character, you might look at their reputation in the industry, track record for fulfilling obligations, and management style. It is also important to get to know the borrower before you enter a deal so that you can get an overall perception of the investor first-hand.

Another way you can learn more about the character of a borrower is to check out their social media pages. It may sound funny, but you can learn a lot about a person by looking at their Facebook, Instagram, Twitter and other social media account profiles. They give you a glimpse into what the borrower values and most importantly, insight into their behaviors and ethics. Take what you find there with a grain of salt. Just because someone shares a funny cat video doesn't mean they are not professional. However, if you find something that concerns you, you may want to investigate a little further by talking to the borrower directly.

TRUST BUT VERIFY

In the end, you want to make sure that you trust the borrower. Most of the time, the borrower may not be someone that you have had the opportunity to build a deep relationship with. Therefore, it is important to meet with the borrower and get to know more about them before you invest. Take your first impressions and overall perception of the borrower into consideration when determining whether or not they seem knowledgeable, trustworthy, and able to repay the loan.

That being said, you still need to do your research. I say, "trust but verify" when you need to go on more than just a gut reaction to decide which borrowers are the right fit. If a real estate investor seems trustworthy and appears to be the ideal borrower, you still need to verify their information to make sure that their past experiences line up with what they are claiming to be true. Looking into all the factors that we've previously discussed will help you determine if a borrower is a good fit for you as a private mortgage lender.

FINDING BORROWERS

So we have spent a lot of time discussing how to analyze borrowers, but the question still lingers, where do you find potential borrowers? This is certainly a great question, but the strategies may differ slightly depending on your geography.

The most common way to find active real estate investors in your community is by attending real estate networking and training events. In major metropolitan areas, this is easy to do. You can start by searching the National Real Estate Investing Association (REIA) website, Is a great place to start, their domain is here: https://nationalreia.org. You can use the search function to find the closest REIA in your area. For example, in a city like Houston where I reside and invest, there are real estate investing networking events almost every night of the week, Monday thru Friday. We host our own networking event every month that draws crowds of around 150 people. You can check out our networking event website at www.ReiAction.com. To find out if there are networking events in your area, you'll want to do some research online. If you find some, you'll want to add their meetings to your calendar and begin attending, networking and meeting with potential borrowers.

Another way to find potential borrowers is by speaking with companies and professionals that may have real estate investors as clients and see if they can provide you with any contact information. You can of course add into the conversation a potential added benefit for their referral. If you are providing financing for additional deals for the investor, then that is also potentially more business for them! Here are some ideas of local professionals you can contact to inquire if they have any reputable real estate investors as clients that may need financing for some of their deals:

- Realtors
- Accountants
- General Contractors
- Real Estate Attorneys
- Insurance Agents

Another strategy to find qualified borrowers is to network and meet other private lenders in your area. This will not only help you to build a network of other lenders who can help you and give you advice, but they may also be able to provide referrals for qualified borrowers who are looking for loan funds. Talk to other private lenders to find out how they identify qualified borrowers or find out about new deals. They may even pass deals onto you that they aren't able to fund at the time.

Another way to locate qualified borrowers is to find experienced investment companies with a track record of successful deals. You can often find these companies through online advertising, their professional website, or other marketing materials. For instance, my company's website explains a lot about who we are and what types of services we provide. This helps potential private lenders better understand who they are investing with.

CHAPTER TAKEAWAYS

If you want to be a successful private mortgage lender, it's vital that you take the time to analyze your borrowers to determine if they are the right fit for you. This requires some research and due diligence efforts into their experience, business model, financials and references. The more effort you put into analyzing your borrower, the more likely you are to have a positive experience as a lender.

Be sure to visit the
Private Lender Playbook page
to access valuable tools & resources

www.PrivateLenderPlaybook.com

Chapter 7: How to Analyze a Deal

> *"The liabilities are always 100 percent good. It's the assets you have to worry about."*
>
> *– Charlie Munger*

Once you have decided what types of investments you want to make and you've found potential borrowers, it's time to analyze the deal to see if it's a worthwhile investment. Analyzing an actual deal requires some work required on your part, but it will be worth it in the end. Doing this work upfront allows you to be confident in your investment and helps you prevent surprises or issues down the road.

In this chapter, I'll take you through the process of how to analyze a deal. I'll start off by explaining different valuation methods and give you some tips for effective analysis so that you will have the best opportunity to choose the right deals for your investment goals. Before we start, I would like to share a brief description and general idea of what a 'deal' actually looks like and provide a free resource to help you analyze potential deals from your borrowers.

DEAL FORMULA

When I coach and train my students real estate investing to flip houses, I have them use a very simple formula to determine if they should proceed with a deal. At a minimum, this typically requires my students to have at least 25% equity in the deal after their purchase price and repair costs. I want to stress that 25% is the minimum acceptable amount of equity for a potential flip deal, and sometimes based on other circumstances (taxes, days on market, etc.), is still not a great deal. It may be good, just not great. Ideally, they are acquiring deals with 27-30% equity before proceeding forward. Let me first share the formula I teach to my students to apply, using the example of a home that would be worth $100,000 after it was completely renovated and updated:

After Repair Value (ARV) of Home = $100,000
Repair Costs: $25,000
Investor's Maximum Offer Price: $50,000
Total Investment of Purchase & Repairs = $75,000 (75% of ARV)

Another way to look at that would be:

$75,000 (75% ARV, of $100,000)
- $25,000 (Repair Costs)
$50,000 Maximum Offer (MO)

This means the maximum allowable offer for an investor to make would be $50,000 because after they factor in the repair cost of $25,000, they will have $75,000 invested into the property.

So as a lender, you could look at it like this:

$75,000 (75% ARV, of $100,000)
- $25,000 (Repair Costs)
$50,000 Investor Maximum Offer (MO)
$75,000 Loan Amount

Therefore, if someone brings you a potential lending deal in which the ARV is going to be $100,000 after all repairs are complete, and it needs $25,000 in repairs, in order to have 25% equity in the deal, you would keep your loan amount to a maximum of $75,000, or a 75% Loan To Value (LTV) ratio.

A question you will certainly have to face as you progress as a private lender, is should you loan on deals that do not meet the 25% equity rule? The 25% equity standard has been an accepted and used ratio for many years, and it provides a nice profit margin with room for error. As a real estate investor and coach to others, this is a proven formula that I've personally used for over a decade to determine if a house is a deal or not, and it's very simple to use. I also happen to invest in the Texas market and I understand that all markets are different, but I would not be doing private money lenders justice if I suggested you should never breach this formula for any flip projects.

There are a few exceptions we run across in some rental property investments and owner finance deals where the numbers still make sense with slightly less equity, but of course, make sure you understand the deal and your borrower to ensure your investment will not be lacking an acceptable amount of equity should the property ever come back to you. Especially for new lenders, the formula of 75% of ARV - Repairs, or 75% LTV, is a great 'safety' zone to stay in as you start your lending journey. As you gain more knowledge and experience, you can begin to navigate more freely and determine your own risk versus reward threshold.

And in practice, most of the deals that our company purchases typically have closer to 30% equity in them. There is no rule saying you as a lender cannot require more equity in the deal, because you absolutely can. And if there is a deal that doesn't have at least 25% equity in it, the simple solution is to require the investor to bring some of their own cash to the closing to make sure you meet that criteria.

Just to be safe, I want to reinforce that using this formula is absolutely critical when you're first getting started. If your loan amount exceeds 75% of the ARV, you are putting yourself at risk because once that line is breached, it becomes more likely your borrower is not going to make a profit, which makes you more susceptible to take a property back. My hope is that you will not become emotionally persuaded when looking at potential lending opportunities and base your decisions on proven lending guidelines. If you choose to go above that 75% LTV range, just make sure you've really done your homework before moving forward.

If you would like to analyze your potential lending deals, I created a free resource many years ago called the Free Flip Analyzer. Feel free to check it out on our resources area of www.PrivateLenderPlaybook.com.

COLLATERAL VALUATION

The first step in analyzing a deal is to understand the value of the loan's underlying collateral. Collateral valuation is important to your overall security and participation in the transaction. This is where you have the opportunity to mitigate risk by determining which properties are worthwhile investments, and which ones make sense when it comes to the numbers as those properties are more uncertain and risky.

In order to effectively determine the value for the collateral, you will want to use several sources to make your evaluation. With several sources confirming the estimated property value, you can feel safer in your investments. Below, I will dive into a few of the methods for valuation.

COMPARATIVE MARKET ANALYSIS (CMA)

The comparative market analysis, or CMA, is a process that you can use to determine the value of the investment property. To conduct a CMA, you will look at recently sold properties in the same geographical area that are similar to the property in question. You will want to compare these properties to the investment property under analysis and adjust for feature differences to come up with an estimated value for the property in question. If you are not a licensed realtor, you will need a realtor familiar with the area to provide the CMA report for you to analyze.

You can also compare the investment property to similar properties in the area that are currently on the market. This allows you to see what the value may potentially be when it goes to market and it can also give you an idea of whether the home value might increase or decrease in the future. This is based on the values of the sold properties as compared to those currently for sale. It should be noted that homes that haven't actually sold are only viewed with a 'grain of salt' and not used for the true valuation. Only properties that have actually sold should be used to formulate the value of the prospective property.

Finding the most relevant comparable properties is a crucial part of determining an accurate market value in your CMA. For example, if investors choose even just one different comparable property out of a few options, they could come up with very different valuations. When choosing comparable properties, pay attention to the following factors:

Property Sale Date – A property that was sold more than two or three months in the past may not be a good comp, especially in markets that are moving very fast. When available, you will want to choose more recent sales to reduce the chance of irrelevant prices in your CMA.

Property Location – It's not always possible to find similar homes recently sold in the same subdivision as the investment property. However, you want to make sure that you're looking at comps in the same general area or neighborhood. If you are not able to find comparable properties there, look for similar homes in similar subdivisions that are in different parts of town, but just use caution because different subdivisions and areas of town can be drastically different in price.

Home Characteristics – You want your comps to be as similar as possible to the property in question. Look for homes with the same or similar features and quantities for items like:

- number of bedrooms and baths
- square footage
- lot size
- Age of construction
- School District

Unfortunately, it is not always possible to find comparable homes that have the same or even similar features as the property in question. When this happens, you will need to make value adjustments to compensate for the differences in the properties. For instance, if the comp has one less bedroom than the investment property, you would assume that it would have sold for more money with an extra bedroom. Therefore, you would adjust the sold price by adding on the value of an extra bedroom.

Many newbie investors and lenders make the mistake of using the tax records to determine the property value. Tax records have no bearing on the true value of a home nor do currently listed prices of homes for sale. You should always remember the numbers can only be considered comparable once the properties being compared have already been sold.

Remember, if you are lending to a borrower who is investing in fix and flip properties, you will need to determine what the value will likely be after all planned renovations have been completed. For instance, if the investor plans to renovate the kitchen and bathrooms, you might look at the property values of similar homes that also have these updated features. It is especially important to consider any room additions that will be included in the rehab, as extra bedrooms and bathrooms can significantly affect the final selling price.

APPRAISALS

There are two general types of appraisals – full appraisals and desktop appraisals. Both types of appraisals are similar in terms of their research and comparable selection, but they do have their differences as well. It's important to understand the difference between the two so that you can make sure you get the right appraisal for your needs.

With a full appraisal, the appraiser visits the home, takes photos and measurements, and evaluates the condition of the property in person. The appraiser needs to see the interior of the home in order to get a more accurate valuation as these factors impact the final value.

A desktop appraisal is performed without a physical inspection of the investment property. The appraiser does all the necessary research right from their desk via the internet and the multiple listing service (MLS). The desktop appraisal can be a more affordable option and will generally suffice to get a very solid valuation for the property.

If you are lending on a property that is out of your area or out of state, or you just aren't sure about the value, don't hesitate to order an appraisal to confirm the value. By practice, I've found desktop appraisals are very accurate and affordable. Due to the cost savings, I would recommend a desktop appraisal if you are considering lending on a fix and flip or rental property and you are uncertain of the value of the prospective property. Though the final selling price will depend on the quality of the renovations that are done, it is important for private lenders to know the value of the property prior to renovations as well as the ARV. Therefore, if something were to go wrong or the investor is not able to complete all the rehabbing he or she has planned, the lender will still have a good idea of the property's worth in its 'as-is' condition.

Sometimes spending the money upfront for a full or desktop appraisal will help save time and heartache later on. When it comes to appraisal costs, you will need to determine who pays for the appraisal – you or the real estate investor. There is no set rule on this so you will want to discuss this ahead of time with the investor. You may even decide to split the cost of the appraisal.

Broker's Price Opinion (BPO)

The broker's price opinion, or BPO, is a process that is similar to an appraisal, but not as complex or involved and typically cheaper in cost. They are often associated with short sales or foreclosures. However, some relocation firms use BPOs to determine the value of a property.

With a BPO, the lender or investor hires a real estate broker to prepare an opinion of value. The broker's representative, who is usually a real estate agent, will compare a minimum of three properties that have recently sold that are similar to the investment property. The representative will adjust the price to account for differences, and the final result is the opinion of market value.

There are two general types of BPOs – the interior BPO and the drive-by BPO. With the interior BPO, the agent will look at the inside of the house as well as the exterior. However, with the drive-by BPO, the agent will only look at the exterior of the home to make a valuation. Sometimes drive-by BPOs are also developed using specialized software that's similar to the estimate that you will find on Zillow.com.

BPOs are typically the least expensive option, and they offer yet another way to determine the approximate value of investment property. In the end, the more options you have for determining the value, the safer you can feel about your investment.

DRIVE THE COMPS

It's a common mantra among private mortgage lenders and lenders alike to "drive the comps" yourself. This means that if you live nearby, don't just look at photos on the appraisal and assume you have determined an accurate property value. Instead, take the appraisal, get into your car, and drive to the property in question to take a look for yourself. You will also want to drive by the comparable properties to see how similar they really are and just confirm the data to give you an extra layer of peace of mind before proceeding with the deal.

CHAPTER TAKEAWAYS

Though getting an accurate value for an investment property takes some time, resources, and work, it is worth all the trouble when it comes down to determining an accurate value for any potential lending opportunity. While there are many different methods that you can use to confirm the valuation of the property in question, all that matters is that you use the best option that works for you and provides accurate results. Don't be afraid to use multiple sources in order to feel confident that the numbers are accurate.

Any effort and time you spend determining property values can be considered time well spent and this is truly one of the fundamentals of a successful private lender in order to properly verify that you have an acceptable amount of equity in each and every deal. And of course, always use proven lending guidelines and formulas to assure that you have an acceptable amount of equity in every deal that you lend on.

Chapter 8: How to Determine Your Interest Rates and Fees

"An investment in knowledge pays the best interest."

– Benjamin Franklin

One of the questions I get most often from new private mortgage lenders is, "how do I determine my interest rates and fees"? In this chapter, we will discuss what some of the typical interest rates and point structures are for many private loans so that you can get a better idea of what other private mortgage lenders are charging. I will also discuss some important factors to consider when setting your interest rates in regard to your investment goals and the investor's experience. While there is not one magical number that every private lender can use as an interest rate or a set number for fees, you can determine what rates and fees work best for you based on the circumstances of the deal and your own personal investment goals. It should also be noted that rates may also be affected by the particular market that you are investing.

INTEREST RATES

It is important to look at your particular market and see what interest rates other private lenders are receiving. As a new private mortgage lender, you will want to network and speak with other lenders and investors in the community to find out what the going rate is in your particular area. Just like running any other type of business, private mortgage lenders can look at the competition's offering to ensure that they are not over or undercharging for their own loan terms. You may find rates of return vary widely from 6 - 18 percent interest depending on the terms of loan, with variables including loan to value ratio, type of loan, borrowers experience/financials, exit strategy, and other miscellaneous factors. It's fairly safe to say that the returns that private mortgage lenders earn easily outperform most other typical investments. Typically, the private lenders that we work with earn between 6 - 10% interest on their loans. But remember, as a private lender, you are the one that establishes the interest rate your borrower's will pay and this is going be based on the market your in, the borrower's experience and the type of investment.

That being said, another thing to consider when setting the interest rate is simply the amount the real estate investor is willing to pay. Sure, all investors want the lowest interest rate possible on their loan. That doesn't mean you should provide the lowest interest rates just to get their business. If your interest rates are too low, you may be missing out on the opportunity to put your money to work at its maximum capacity. But, if you're rates are too high, you may end up losing out on a deal that could have worked out well for both you and the investor.

Furthermore, you do need to consider what a reasonable interest rate looks like based on the type of loan (short or long-term), the loan amount, the risk involved, and perhaps most importantly, the experience of the investor. While there are investors out there who will pay up to 12 or even 18% interest, these borrowers tend to carry extra risk. Less experienced real estate investors will often pay more for their loan. However, you need to consider whether the higher interest is worth the additional risk that you will be taking on.

To put this into perspective for you, my company places private lenders' capital with our deals with the least expensive money available. Our experience and history of success shows our lenders we know what we are doing, and therefore working with us carries less risk than working with someone who is less experienced. While I might have paid more for loans when I was first getting started, we are fortunate to have lending relationships with rates and terms much more flexible and less expensive than many of our competitors.

In the end, when it comes to establishing interest rates, a question that I like to ask new private lenders is – "What rate of return would you be happy with?". I like to start with this open ended question to work toward a 'win-win' relationship. For instance, if the investor is very happy with a 6 - 8% return for example, compared to their 1% savings account return, it's often easy to deploy their capital to one of our deals or one of my real estate coaching students' deals very quickly. But if the lender is seeking a return in the 12%+ range, then I encourage them to continue looking for a borrower they trust they can place their money with at that rate.

In this instance, their money could have possibly been invested and consistently earning a 6 - 8%, however, because they were seeking the higher rate, their money may remain 'stale', uninvested and not working for them. I see this happen very often from conversations that I have with prospective lenders. The story of tortoise and the hare often comes to mind! Over and over again, I talk to new lenders that are seeking interest rates in the 12% or higher range, yet when I talk to them 3, 6, or even 9 months later, their capital is still not deployed. From what I recall, the slow and steady pace of the tortoise eventually wins the race.

This is simply something for you to consider with your investment strategy and rate of returns you are seeking. If you have the relationships and network to consistently earn 12% or higher returns from investors whom you feel comfortable investing with, then by all means, move forward. But if you find yourself in a situation where your money is typically parked and not being invested, consider reduced rates of return in order to get your money working for you.

ORIGINATION POINTS OR FEES

On average, private mortgage lenders will charge between 1 to 2 origination points, or 1% to 2% of the loan amount, as fees. Again, you want to stay within the general range when determining the points for your private mortgage loans. Some private mortgage lenders will choose not to charge any fees and just collect on the interest. Just as with setting the interest rate, you will want to consider what other lenders in the market are charging for fees and what the borrower is willing to pay.

In fact, many of my lenders will waive their origination points so that they can be more competitive in the marketplace. It allows them to get their money working for them quicker and more often, which is the ultimate goal. Just like homeowners shop mortgage brokers for bank loans, real estate investors will do the same to look for the best deals available when looking for private loans.

However, as a word of caution, private mortgage lenders need to be careful and try to avoid being too greedy by charging excessive fees as this could cause them to lose out on a deal. It is important to consider that the real estate investor is also concerned about getting a return on their own investment, so experienced investors will typically not accept unreasonably high interest rates or fees if they have less expensive options. In the end, you don't want to miss out on a great investment opportunity due to the fact that you priced yourself out by 1% or 2% on an excellent lending opportunity.

SHORT VS. LONG-TERM

We discussed this earlier, but I want to bring up the topic again on short vs. long-term deals. One thing you need to consider when determining your interest rates and fees on private loans is whether you are investing in long or short-term deals. Ultimately, your decisions will depend on your overall investment goals and risk tolerance. However, it is worth reiterating here because the interest rates and fees will change depending on whether you are offering a loan with a longer or shorter payback period.

Private lenders can charge higher interest rates for short-term fix and flip deals. However, these deals carry more risk, and their short-term nature requires you to do a little more work to continuously find new investors and deals. On the other hand, long-term deals are typically less risky and allows you to make consistent income over time. With a long-term deal like a rental property, you are not faced with the daunting task of continuously finding new investors. Though short-term deals may initially seem more attractive to the private money lender because of the potential for higher interest rates, long-term deals allow you to get more out of your investment in the long-run.

It's just like the story of the tortoise and the hare that I mentioned earlier. Even though the hare is incredibly fast, the hare will inevitably lose the race against the tortoise who applies the methodology of being consistent and steady, which eventually helps win the race. The same methodology applies here to long-term investors. I see a lot of investors who want to charge a higher interest rate so they can earn more money faster. However, their money is not working nearly as frequently as an investor who is thinking about the long-term and seeking a lower interest rate. When investors try to earn higher rates, they find themselves in a predicament when their money is sitting for long periods of time because they are always having to look for new ways to invest. Just make sure you find the most effective and profitable balance for you with your rates and fees.

When I talk to private lenders who are enticed by the idea of higher interest rates, I use an return on investment (ROI) spreadsheet to show them a comparison of a low-risk versus high-risk investments. Typically, a long-term low-risk investment strategy with an interest rate 7% continually working month to month will outperform a 10-12% investment simply because the lower interest investment tends to stay 'working' much longer. Many times 10-12% investments are very short-term loans so their capital may only be invested, on average, for 6 to 8 months out of the year. Often, private lenders will find they will make just as much, if not more, with their money consistently working than they would with short-term deals that offered higher interest. Additionally, with a long-term, lower risk investing strategy, you are making income that's more passive rather than having to constantly analyze deals, analyze new borrowers and take on additional risks.

In the end, you need to choose the investment type and corresponding interest rate that makes the most sense for your individual financial goals. If you decide to invest in short-term deals, then you can undoubtedly earn higher rates of return. However, make sure you adjust your interest rates for long-term deals like rental properties and keep a close ear to the ground to hear what is going on in your local market.

DON'T LOSE THE DEAL

Like I mentioned before, don't make the mistake many private mortgage lenders do and price yourself out of opportunities by charging too much for the loan, especially those who are new to the industry and learning how to set rates. The saying I mentioned before – "you can tell the experience of an investor by what they are willing to pay for their money" – applies here. While new real estate investors are willing to accept higher interest rates in an effort to gain more experience and build a history of loan repayment, more experienced investors will not pay as much for their private loans.

However, experienced investors are more likely to follow through on their obligations and successfully finish deals. You don't want to lose a potentially great deal with an experienced investor due to overpricing. Similarly, you don't want to miss out on the opportunity to work and build a relationship with a successful real estate investor because you have priced yourself out of the opportunity. That's why it is vital to consider the experience level of the potential investor before setting the interest rate.

Chapter Takeaways

Just as the conditions of each loan will change with every deal, so will the interest rate and fees associated with each loan. The key to finding the right interest rate and fees is arriving at a number that allows you to make money, fits well within the market average, and is acceptable to yourself and the borrower. The bottom line is this, you should seek to find the interest rates and terms that serves you and your investment plan. At the same time, monitor your results to assure that your money is consistently at work for you in the market producing profitable returns, with trustworthy investors and minimizing risks.

Chapter 9: The People and the Process

"The most expensive advice in the world is free advice"

– Robert Kiyosaki

Trust me, there's a lot more to private lending than just doing some online research and having the borrower sign paperwork. Before you start lending money as a private mortgage lender, it's important that you understand the details that need to take place prior to closing and funding a deal. By getting to know and understand the steps, as well as who is involved during each stage, you can make sure that you're taking the right course toward minimizing risks in your investment.

This chapter will go more in depth on what the private lending steps looks like. I'll discuss each party involved in the process and provide more details on the role that each person plays in moving forward with the loan. I'll also talk a little bit about what happens before and after the borrower signs the loan documents.

PARTIES INVOLVED

Before we dive further into some of the procedures that will need to take place, let's take a look at all of the parties that are involved with loan closing and funding.

BORROWER

This is the individual or entity that is borrowing money against the real estate asset they are trying to purchase. If an individual is acting on behalf of a business as a limited liability company (LLC), then this person will have a resolution that grants them authority to act on behalf of the entity. In other words, they need proof they are able to borrow on behalf of the company they represent.

As I discussed in an earlier chapter, you as a private mortgage lender will have already analyzed the borrower to determine whether or not you would like to invest with them. In addition to credit history, business experience, and trustworthiness, you'll also want to make sure their investment strategies fit in with your own investment goals.

SELLER (FOR PURCHASE TRANSACTIONS)

The seller will also be a part of the process for purchase transactions. This is the individual or entity that is selling the property to the buyer. The seller will have previously agreed to a purchase price with the buyer and they will receive proceeds for the property after all items in the closing transaction are signed and completed to the private lender's satisfaction.

You (As the Private Money Lender)

As a private mortgage lender, obviously you are an integral part of the loan and closing process. You are providing the funds necessary for the borrower to buy the property from the seller. As the private lender, you will come to an agreement with the borrower regarding principal amount, interest rate, fees, loan repayment terms and other particulars about your agreement.

Licensed Real Estate Agent

Depending on the transaction, a real estate agent or multiple agents may also be a part of the contract. A licensed real estate agent who represents either the borrower or the seller may be present in order to negotiate sales terms in the contract. In addition to showing the house and marketing the property, the seller's agent may also negotiate with buyers to determine a final selling price. While the buyer's agent may have had a hand in finding the investment property for the buyer, the real estate agent may also be involved in negotiations and contract terms.

Licensed Real Estate Attorney

Believe it or not, some real estate investors don't use an attorney to prepare their loan documents and they actually prepare their own documents! Proceed with caution if you are lending to an investor that is preparing their own loan documents without the help of a qualified real estate attorney, or better yet, don't proceed at all! Plain and simple, the best way to reduce risk and help make sure that your investment is secure, work with a licensed and experienced real estate attorney that you trust to prepare all documentation. I would encourage you to verify the attorney's background to determine if they are in good standing with the state bar association and they have a specialization in real estate.

Our company always uses an experienced, licensed real estate attorney to prepare all loan documents and to review title commitments and any other necessary documentation. This is the best way that we can ensure all documents are drafted properly for both our company as investors and for the sake of our private lenders.

As a matter of fact, we actually use a "Lenders Attorney", meaning our docs are drawn up to favor our lenders over us as the borrowers. When it comes to buying and selling property, a real estate attorney can either represent the buyer or the seller. It is the same way for preparing loan documents. Attorneys can either represent the lender or the borrower. We made the decision a long time ago to have our attorneys draw up the loan documents on our lenders behalf to give them another layer of peace of mind while investing with our company.

TITLE COMPANY

In most western states in the U.S., title and escrow are performed by two different departments within the same company. However, in the eastern states, escrow is referred to as 'settlement services' and these tasks are performed by an attorney. Note: We will be also be referring to independent escrow companies or settlement service providers as "title company" in this book. However, the terminology will vary based on which state you operate.

The title company acts as a neutral third party who will collect and disburse funds for the parties involved in the transaction, based on your instructions. They also oversee the signing of applicable loan and legal documents. And finally, they will record the finalized documents with the county office. But let's discuss further about our friends at the title company.

The title company also provides a preliminary title report, aka a Title Commitment, for the property being offered as collateral for the loan. The title insurance company compiles this report by searching county public records for information such as liens, judgments, easements, restrictions and anything else against the property, the borrower and seller. The private mortgage lender can use this information to determine whether the property can be insured. If the property's title can be insured, then the transaction will continue and the title company will disclose pricing to issue a title policy of insurance.

It is important to note that all private mortgage lenders should work with an experienced attorney when drafting or reviewing the title instructions. There is more to title insurance than there is to homeowners insurance. With homeowners insurance, you typically have a few basic choices to make, like the deductible options and amount of coverage. However, when it comes to title insurance, there are two types of title policies and various endorsements. Title insurance is an indemnity insurance, which means it will only protect the policyholder from financial loss sustained from defects in a title to a property. That's why it's beneficial to have an experienced attorney help guide you through this paperwork to ensure that you're minimizing risk and protecting your investment.

As an extra precaution, our company policy is to always provide our private lenders a loan title policy. This type of policy insures that the lender is protected with additional security for providing mortgage funds to the real estate investor or buyer. A loan title policy does not protect the buyer. However, it does protect the lender in the event the seller was not legally able to transfer their ownership rights. Our company includes and pays for this type of title policy on every transaction in order to provide a better and more secured investing experience for our private lenders and in my opinion, you should require the same.

CLOSING COORDINATOR

Some of the larger and more professional real estate investing companies will also enlist the services of a closing coordinator. The closing coordinator assists and supports the buyer, seller, and the title company throughout the closing process to ensure that everything goes smoothly.

Our company employs a full-time closing coordinator who works to confirm that everything is taken care of properly from start to finish. Our closing coordinator checks to make sure that all the 'I's are dotted and the T's are crossed' so there are no issues or surprises during the closing process. This not only helps us feel confident that everything is right on our end, but it also ensures that our private lenders have a positive experience when working with us.

Our closing coordinator has over 30+ years' experience in the title business so this adds tremendous leverage to our company and our lenders. And while I understand that most investors that you work with won't have a closing coordinator, many companies similar or larger in size to ours do. Either way, the important thing is to make sure you have someone you can contact with any questions you may have about the title commitment you are receiving. Your real estate attorney will typically be the best person to contact for any questions you have during this stage of the lending process.

What Happens Before the Borrower Signs the Loan Documents?

The one item that starts this whole process is a signed contract and agreement between the seller and the buyer to sell the property at a certain amount. For example, if the seller has accepted the buyer's request to purchase the property for $100,000, then they will enter into a legal agreement/contract that states this and any other pertinent details regarding the transaction. The real estate investor (or borrower) will then make a loan request, either verbally or in writing, to the private lender to borrow the amount of money they need for the property. In this example, they might request to borrow $100,000 to purchase the property and $25,000 for repairs. The parties will then deposit earnest money with the title company to get the ball rolling.

Once the borrower and the private lender have an agreement regarding the principal and loan terms, they will communicate their agreement to the licensed real estate attorney, and the attorney will begin preparing the loan documents. After the loan documents are prepared, but before the borrower signs any loan documents, the investor must set some things into action. First, the investor or their real estate agent will order a title search to get the closing process started.

The title company will then gather all the information they need from the seller and the borrower. They will conduct a search of county records to look for liens, judgments, easements, etc. against the property, the borrower, and the seller. The title company will then create a preliminary title report/commitment that serves as an offer of title insurance for the property.

The title company will review any organizational documents from the people or entities involved in the transaction and determine who needs to sign the documents. The title company will also obtain payoffs of existing liens on the property. If applicable, they will also obtain leases, rent rolls, service contracts, property tax info, security deposits, and anything else that is necessary for proration calculations.

Once all requirements are taken care of, the title company will prepare settlement statements that are in line with both your instructions and the purchase contract after receiving the loan document package from the private lender. The last task for the title or escrow company is to coordinate and oversee the actual signing of the documents. This is the final step in the loan closing process.

What Happens After the Borrower Signs the Loan Documents?

After the borrower has signed the loan documents, it's time for you to fund their loan. As the lender, you will be the one to wire the monies that you provide to the title company. The title company will be recording the deed, mortgage, and any other documents with the appropriate county offices. The title company will then disburse the required funds to appropriate parties. Finally, the title company will issue the title insurance policies once the recording process is complete.

Once the security documents are recorded, such as the mortgage or trust deed and the funds have been disbursed, the loan transaction is considered complete. The entire length of the funding and closing process will vary based on state laws and county processes, which differ from region to region. Typically, many states require documents to be signed and funds disbursed the same day or no later than three days of the loan documents being signed and all other requirements being satisfied.

Before we close this chapter out, I want to stress that you never want to lend funds directly to an investor. You should always require title company closings and all funding to go through your title company to make sure that everything is above board and all of the proper documents are prepared, signed and recorded properly.

Chapter Takeaways

Though it can sometimes seem overwhelming for new private mortgage lenders, the truth is that the process is easier than you think. Keep the following in mind as you get started taking on the role of being a private mortgage lender:

- The borrower, seller, private mortgage lender, real estate agent, and title company all have their roles to play in the lending process.
- Working with an experienced attorney can help you better understand proper loan documentation and title insurance to make sure that your investment is protected.
- The more effort you put into understanding the lending process and the role that each player takes on, the better you will be able to minimize the risks in your investment.

By speaking with qualified experts like local real estate attorneys and accountants, you can work to build a strong team that will help guide you through the process.

Now that you know what the lending process looks like, you may be curious about what types of loan documents are required. Fear not! That is exactly what we will be covering in the next chapter.

Be sure to visit the
Private Lender Playbook page
to access valuable tools & resources

www.PrivateLenderPlaybook.com

Chapter 10: Loan Documentation and Securing Your Investment

"I am more concerned with the return of my money than the return on my money."

— Will Rogers

Loan documentation is a vital part of the private lending process. Getting the right documentation in place is essential to securing your investment. It allows you to solidify the verbal agreement that you already have in place with the borrower and helps to keep everyone on the same page and honest about the loan terms. Without loan documentation, you are not able to hold borrowers accountable for holding up their end of the deal.

Even though an experienced real estate attorney will help you make sure you have all your bases covered when it comes to documentation, it's important for private mortgage lenders to understand what type of documentation is required and how each specific document helps secure the investment. In this chapter, I'm going to cover why loan documentation is so important and how each type of document works to secure your investment.

WHY LOAN DOCUMENTATION IS IMPORTANT

Though it may be obvious to some, it is important to have documentation for your private loans. A surprising amount of loans are completed each and every year with nothing more than a home-made contract between the borrower and the lender, and nothing else. Obviously, this is a recipe for disaster. So I believe it is worthwhile to cover what is considered the proper loan documents to require as well as to explain why private loan documentation should be taken seriously as a vital part of the private lending process.

Plain and simple, any loan that you enter into as a private lender should be well-documented and secured by paperwork from a real estate attorney. An effective, properly constructed loan agreement will put everything that has been discussed or agreed to verbally into a written document. By putting everything into writing, you are making sure each party has clear expectations. This leaves less room for potential surprises down the road. After several years of a loan being in place, without clear loan documents, you or the borrower may forget what you had initially agreed to when working toward a loan agreement. However, a written document has a much better memory, so to speak. It serves as a record of what you (as the lender) and the borrower have discussed and agreed to. This helps to make sure everyone is on the same page and ensures you and the borrower maintain a positive working relationship.

Not only does proper documentation help keep your professional relationships intact, it also protects each party in a private mortgage. Remember, you don't know what you don't know about the future. It is best to avoid any legal loose ends from the start by making sure you have all the proper paperwork in place from the very beginning. Last and certainly not least, having proper loan documentation and recording, places you in the most favorable position in the event you must foreclose on the borrower and take the property back.

As you review your agreement, it is important you make sure every conceivable detail is spelled out so there are no questions regarding what is expected from both you and the borrower. Make sure you answer the following questions:

- When are payments due?
- What if payments are not received?
- How and where should payments be made?
- Can the borrower prepay, and is there a penalty for doing so?
- Is the loan secured with any collateral?
- What can the lender do if the borrower misses payments?
- Is the borrower offering a Personal Guarantee?

This is just a starting point for making sure you have covered all your bases in the written documentation. Though it may seem overwhelming at first, don't worry. An experienced real estate attorney will cover these questions for you in their documentation preparation. However, as I said before, it is important that you verify all the information is there and spelled out in great detail.

Standard Private Loan Documentation

It is critical as a private lender that you document the loan by creating the appropriate security documents and disclosures to the borrower. There are many state and federal regulations you will need to follow for proper documentation. If you violate these regulations, this can invalidate the loan, which may result in lost interest and fees. Therefore, it is vital that you work with the appropriate professionals, like a real estate attorney, and seek guidance along the way to make sure that your paperwork is in order before lending any money to an investor.

Your real estate attorney will help prepare this documentation and make sure everything is in place to help you secure your investment. However, it is important for you to understand what each document is about. This not only offers a peace of mind for you as an investor, but it will also make it easier for you to verify you have everything you need in place before closing.

Promissory Note

A promissory note is basically a signed document that says the borrower promises to pay money to a specific person. This serves as written evidence of the debt amount, the repayment terms and schedule, and the interest rate. It is sort of like a contract as it outlines the loan terms that you and the borrower have agreed to.

MORTGAGE OR DEED OF TRUST

A deed of trust, is a document that helps secure the lender's investment to the property. It is a security document where the legal rights to a property are transferred to a trustee, or the person who is given administrative control of the property with the legal obligation to administer it for the specified purposes. The trustee holds the property as security for the loan or debt between the borrower and lender. The equitable title will remain with the borrower.

The deed of trust is the same document the bank uses during the lending process to secure their investment. This document is what will allow you as the private lender to legally foreclose on the property if the borrower does not make their payments. This document also provides some security in your investment as it gives you legal recourse should the borrower not hold up their end of the deal.

Often, people will refer to a home loan as a "mortgage," but the mortgage is not actually a loan. The mortgage is a document that the borrower gives to the lender to create a lien on the property in question. Certain states will refer to this as a mortgage while others will refer to it as a deed of trust.

TITLE INSURANCE

As discussed earlier, title insurance is a form of indemnity insurance that acts as a preventative measure to help protect the buyer. A Lender's Title policy as discussed earlier in the book helps insure your lien position as a lender and offers fraud protection against forgery. The transaction requires a title insurance company or real estate attorney to look through property records to see if there have been any clerical errors, omissions in deeds, unknown liens, or any other mistakes in examining records. This helps verify that the seller owns the property and is able to sell it. If there is a title or public record defect, this needs to be taken care of before closing.

Additionally, it is ideal to have your loan closing performed at a title company to make sure that all of your paperwork is complete and correct before signing and transferring the funds to the borrower. There is typically no cost in closing at a title company as this service is included when the title company is issuing the title insurance, So why not take advantage of this service that has every benefit in the world for you? And by the way, any costs that are incurred are covered by the borrower as a general rule. A reputable title company can be considered a valuable team member as they will help to review all of the affiliated closing documents and forms required for the closing and help to assure that all required items are complete and accurate prior to closing. I would not allow any deal that we purchase to not take place at a title company. This is a non-negotiable rule in my book.

PROPERTY INSURANCE

As a private lender, you must require and verify the borrower has the appropriate fire and liability insurance in the amounts you as the private lender want them to have. Always verify the policy is in place prior to closing. You will need to require the insurance company be notified to include you as the "loss payee" on the policy. This will protect you in the event of a loss or damage to the property by ensuring you will be the first one who gets a check. Insurance companies will compensate loss payee's first, before any other payments are released to any other parties. This will ensure your interest is protected and you receive payment for any damage to the property and it also means you will be notified if there is any lapse of coverage or if the borrower is delinquent in payments or moving their policy to another provider. By being named as the loss payee on the insurance policy, you are also able to check in with the insurance company periodically to verify the insurance is still valid. I recommend checking in each quarter just to make sure your investment is still secure.

Insurance can be a cumbersome and complicated subject, so it is well worth your time to place a call to a trusted insurance agent to review a policy on any deals you are lending on to make sure your position is properly protected with the policy the borrower has chosen. Also, having an insurance agent you trust is a useful resource to have any time you have a question that may arise regarding the coverage of any of your deals.

SURVEY

In almost every instance, we order a new Survey prior to purchasing a home. This isn't something all of our lenders require, but it is our internal policy for our company, and I think it is something you should require as well. An exception of when we don't order a survey is when the current seller has a recent survey the title company will accept and insure. In those instances, there is no need to order and pay for a new survey, which typically cost upwards of $500 in our area, and sometimes substantially more for larger pieces of land.

Why is a survey something you should require as a lender? In short, a survey will show the house and any other structures assumed to be a part of the transaction that are located within the property borders. The survey will also show if there are any encroachments on the property from neighbors fencing, driveways, etc. to the extent they affect legal title or use of the property. There are many, many other benefits to requiring a survey. For example, there may be an existing lawful obligation to share a joint driveway with a neighbor. Surveys also typically show the existence of underground drains or cables which may in turn grant a city or utility company the lawful right to access the use of a portion of the property for upkeep of utility lines. On occasion, although extremely rare, surveys may disclose burial grounds and old cemeteries smack dab in the middle of the backyard! Like I said, rare, but still possible!

The bottom line is surveys can greatly affect the value, plans and marketability of the property and most importantly, they help to secure your investment by validating that the property you are loaning on is actually what it was contracted to be. So my advice is to err on the side of caution and require your borrowers to provide a survey on every deal you lend on.

SHOULD I INVEST IN 2ND LIENS?

I would like to close out this chapter with a discussion about investing in second liens and if this is a secure path for you as a private lender. First, let me briefly explain what a second lien is. Basically, a second lien is a loan that is junior or subordinate to the first lien. This essentially equates to lack of control in the property in the event something goes wrong. For example, in the event of a loan default, the second lien holder would only be reimbursed after the superior or senior liens are repaid in full after the sale of the home. Furthermore, the second lien holder may only receive a fraction, if any of their invested loan amount. As you can see, second liens carry substantially more risk than first liens and I will also tell you that many, if not most of my seasoned lending partners will not invest in 2nd lien mortgages, with no exceptions.

While I agree that limiting yourself to only first lien positions is a sound and wise strategy, I will tell you that in our business, we borrow a substantial amount from second lien lenders, and have been doing so for years. You're likely wondering why anyone would invest in a second lien when there are inherently many more risks than a first lien position? This is certainly true so let me explain a few of the reasons why and also share some safeguards if you decide to invest in second/junior liens.

Many second lien lenders simply do not have enough capital to invest in order to secure a full first lien position. Therefore they loan smaller amounts for junior loan positions and typically, but not always, in exchange for higher interest rates because of the increased risk. There are a couple of ways they can help mitigate risks, one critical factor is by only lending to established real estate investors with a proven track record of success. Additionally, even though this is a second lien, they do not allow their loan, in conjunction with the first lien, to exceed the 75% loan to value ratio. Therefore, in the event of default, even being in the second lien position, they are still helping to ensure there will be an acceptable amount of equity.

Another good rule of thumb is to never invest as a second lien unless you have the ability to buy out, or pay off the first lien. This doesn't mean you have to have the cash sitting in the bank, but rather that you need to have the ability to acquire the funds to pay off the first loan either from a bank line of credit, or simply raising the money yourself from your network or some other source of funds. In the event of default, you as the second lien lender would have the ability to payoff the senior lien and be able to take back control of the property. It is also most ideal if you know the superior lien holder and keep an open line of communication with them.

Once again, I am not an attorney so I strongly encourage you to do your proper due diligence before investing in a second lien. In closing, while second liens are a viable option for some, for many others, they are not. Make sure that you utilize the proper safeguards for yourself if you decide to move forward as a private lender with second lien investing.

Chapter Takeaways

If you want to reduce risks and do all that you can to make sure your investment is secure, then proper loan documentation is the best place to start. No one likes paperwork, but proper loan documentation is essential to making sure that each party involved in the deal knows what is expected of them and what they need to do to effectively follow through. This helps to maintain positive working relationships with your borrower while also protecting the money you have invested in the deal.

I cannot reiterate enough just how important it is to work with a team of professionals when drawing up your private loan documents. A qualified and experienced real estate attorney and title company will help you make sure your documentation is created and recorded to protect your investment.

Chapter 11: Construction Repair Draws and Inspections

"Trust, but verify."

– Ronald Reagan

Most often when you are funding a loan, the real estate investor will need capital to purchase the property as well as funds to repair or rehab the property. Whether you are focusing on lending to fix and flip investors or landlord investors, it's important to understand repair draws and what your options are for releasing funds for construction repairs.

There are a few different approaches to repair draws and choosing the right approach will often depend on the deal and your working relationship with the investor. In this chapter, I will cover a few of your options for getting your borrowers the funds they need to rehab the property while also safeguarding your position.

THE BASICS OF REPAIR DRAWS

To explain the basics of repair draws, we'll use an example. Let's say an investor comes to you with a deal that looks something like this – they need $100,000 to purchase the property and $25,000 for repairs. This comes to a total investment of $125,000. If you decide to do business with this investor, then you will need to consider how and when you release the funds to them for the repairs.

I will be very transparent and tell you that typically my lenders will loan 100% of the repair funds and release them at the purchase closing, or in other words, they loan us the repair monies up front. In this example, that would mean the $25,000 for repairs would be released to my company at the time of closing so we could complete the necessary repairs and do so without any repair draws or inspections. However, this agreement is based on my company's positive relationship with our lenders and our long-standing track record of successful rehab projects. It is not something I would advise for anyone reading this book without an established relationship with your borrower.

In almost every conceivable lending situation, you will best secure your investment by instituting a draw schedule to require your borrower to make certain repairs before receiving rehab monies. Repair draws outline what is required for the borrower to get the funds they need for construction repairs and how they get reimbursed after the repairs are completed.

With repair draws, the repair money is set aside, often held in Escrow, and released once the investor has reached certain agreed upon milestones. Repair draws ensure the property is being repaired to a certain standard with all renovations done properly and up to code. Repair draws also ensure that the repair funds requested are being used to complete the repairs previously listed and disclosed to the lender. Since the private loan amount is based on the value of the property after certain repairs are made, it is important the investor makes the repairs they have originally proposed.

Of course, I will note that oftentimes circumstances or 'surprises' can change the course of a rehab project. Due to these surprises, real estate investors will need to make adjustments to the types of improvements or repairs they need to make to the investment property. As long as the modifications are continuing to add value to the property and not affecting your loan to value position, this should not be an issue for you as a private mortgage lender. The most important thing to keep in mind is that any changes in the renovation plans that are made using this allotted money must improve the value of the investment property and your total loan amount has not changed even if the investor goes over their original anticipated budget.

GUIDELINES FOR REPAIR DRAWS

You will need to work with your borrower prior to closing to establish a draw agreement that outlines what repairs need to be done before repair money or escrow can be released to the borrower. This agreement will be communicated to your attorney and included in the loan documents. This pre-determined schedule outlines when the funds will be provided to the borrower and under what conditions. When I personally lend on deals to other investors, I have found it best to require a line-itemized list of repairs that the investor intends to complete. Therefore, you or an inspection company you hire can easily check off each repair or renovation as it is completed and release the funds once the work has been inspected. Too often, inexperienced investors provide vague repair lists that do not outline the specific repairs and their estimated costs. This can make it difficult when it comes time to release the draws. So it is important to ask the investor not just for repair estimates, but also for the cost of each repair, in an itemized format.

Using the example provided above in the previous section, let's discuss what the repair draws might look like. Let's say the subject property requires $25,000 in repairs. You might structure your draws as $10,000 for exterior renovations and $15,000 for interior construction repairs, based on the itemized list the investor has provided. For example, for exterior repairs you might provide $5,000 for siding repairs, $2,500 for painting, $1,500 for landscaping and $1,000 for fencing repairs. If you are planning on reimbursing the borrower (or requiring them to make all the repairs before receiving the repair funds) then they would make the repairs on the exterior and interior. Once these repairs are complete, an inspector will inspect the renovations to make sure that they are done correctly and up to code. Once you are satisfied that the repairs have been done correctly, the funds could then be disbursed to the investor.

In addition to the reimbursement approach, you might instead require the investor to make a certain amount of renovations before releasing all the repair funds. For instance, you could require them to make 30% of the renovations, and then, after inspection, release all $25,000 to complete the necessary repairs. This approach works well for experienced investors who have a history of successful rehab projects. You may already be confident in their ability to successfully make repairs, so this option allows you to check in after 30% of repairs are completed and to make sure that things are going smoothly before you disburse all the funds for construction repairs. Another option is to release some of the funds up-front during the closing process, and then establish more draws later on as the repairs are completed and the property is inspected.

As you build relationships with investors and work with those who have an established history of successful rehab projects, you may then decide to release the funds up front for all construction repairs. If you choose this option, you would disburse the repair funds during the closing process along with the funds used to purchase the property. By doing so, the investor can put the money to work as soon as possible by starting on the repairs. Once again, this is not something that I recommend, but it is what happens in the 'real world' for many lenders and borrowers.

While deciding on the specifics of your repair draws, you will need to consider whether the property will be inspected by an outside party in order to approve the repair draws. If so, you will need to consider the inspection fees in your agreement with the borrower. You will also need to determine who will inspect the property after the repairs are complete and what process they will follow to approve or deny the repairs. Although it is typical that the borrower be responsible for paying the inspections to receive draws (typically around $100 per inspection), you may want to hire an outside party if it is your first time working with an investor to verify the work has been done with acceptable workmanship.

Once again, always be sure to have your real estate attorney document and outline the draw procedures you agreed to with your borrower. This will help protect you while also making sure everyone is on the same page. With clear draw procedures, the borrower knows what guidelines they have to follow and what repairs need to be completed in order for them to get the repair funds that were agreed to.

How to Determine Repair Draws

There is no hard and fast way to determine your repair draw terms. It is important that you consider each deal on its own before deciding when you will disburse the funds for construction repairs. When deciding on terms for repair draws, consider the condition of the property, the estimated value after repairs and the borrower's experience with rehab projects.

For instance, if the real estate investor has a long history of successful rehab projects or you have worked with the investor before, then you may be less concerned about their ability to properly repair the property and use the repair funds appropriately. However, if you have not worked with the investor before or they are new to the realm of rehab, then you may want to consider slowly disbursing the funds to ensure that the repairs are up to acceptable standards and the investor is using the repair funds as they have indicated.

Another factor to consider when lending to new real estate investors is whether or not they have established their team of contractors. Most new investors are still working to put together their team, and the construction industry can be rather 'cut throat'. Unfortunately, if the investor doesn't have experience rehabbing and does not yet have a team of contractors who they trust with a proven track record, they may end up mismanaging the repair funds or paying their contractors up-front for work that has not yet been completed. For newer investors, it makes more sense to establish draws as the work is completed and inspected.

When working with a more experienced investor or investment company that has been in business for many years or decades, you are more likely to find they will know how to manage construction efficiently and already have the contracting team in place to make repairs happen on time and with acceptable quality.

CHAPTER TAKEAWAYS

Working with real estate investors as a private lender will require you to carefully consider how you plan to disburse the repair funds. The right option for you as a lender will depend on the property and investor in question. The borrowers background and experience as well as the deal will all factor into the decision you make on the best structure to secure your investment with. This will also encourage the investors to complete the repairs as quickly as possible without unnecessary delays so they can quickly get their property on the market to sale or lease.

It is important that you work with an experienced real estate attorney when developing your repair draw agreement and schedule. This will help ensure that you do not leave out any important details. It is vital to have a clear and precise agreement so the investor knows what they need to do to successfully receive their repair funds.

So far we have primarily discussed using your cash to invest as a private lender. But in the next chapter, I've invited a close friend of mine to cover how to perform these same investments in your self-directed IRA. Get ready to really learn some exciting information on how to invest in real estate notes tax-free!

Chapter 12: Investing in your Self-Directed IRA

"How many millionaires do you know who have become wealthy by investing in savings accounts? I rest my case."

– Robert G. Allen

The following chapter was contributed by Nathan Long, CEO of Quest IRA.

Hello, my name is Nathan Long and I am the CEO of Quest IRA. All of the accounts offered at Quest IRA are self-directed, meaning you get to make the decisions and our staff will provide expert account administration and transaction support services. As the CEO of Quest IRA, I oversee the operations of the company and aid in continually improving the practices implemented to provide a better experience for our more than 13,000 clients. After joining my brother, Quincy Long, the founder of Quest, and the Quest IRA team in 2007, I have worked to grow the company to almost 100 employees located in multiple cities and states with continued expansion planned for the near future. So what is Quest IRA and what exactly do we do?

Quest IRA, Inc. (www.QuestIRA.com) is a third party administrator of self-directed IRAs in Houston, Austin, and

Dallas, Texas and soon to be in Seattle, Washington. Quest IRA is the leading provider of self-directed retirement account administration services and has been in business since 2003 with over $1 billion in assets under management from our clients. As a neutral party, Quest IRA does not offer any investments and therefore has no conflicts of interest with what clients want to do with their IRAs. We are not CPAs or legal advisors, but rather administrators of IRAs for the purpose of investing in alternative investments, such as real estate, notes, oil and gas, private placements, etc. All of the accounts offered at Quest IRA are self-directed, which means you get to make the decisions and we provide expert account administration and transaction support services. Quest allows you to be in total control of your retirement wealth and we offer continual training and educational classes weekly in our offices and online.

Prior to working at Quest IRA, I was in the automotive industry for over 17 years as an upper level executive for Automotive Investment Group, AIG, and participated in growing the ABC Nissan Branch in Phoenix, Arizona. I also hold a title of Certified IRA Services Professional (CISP), from the Institute of Certified Bankers. Personally, I'm a devout vegan, love animals and have a passion for cooking. In my spare time, you'll likely find me working with rescued animals and travelling with my wife. But that's enough about me and Quest. Let's discuss investing in real estate as a private lender using your Self-Directed IRA and learn how to do so tax free!

I will assume that since you're reading this book, then you already know that education is the key to investing. Learning how to use a Self-Directed IRA (SDIRA) and understanding the rules and responsibilities that come along with it can benefit you as an investor. Many people don't even know what a Self-Directed IRA is and may not be aware they can self-direct their retirement by doing real estate deals or creating loans between private lenders and borrowers. At Quest, we provide a tremendous amount of free education and training to help SDIRA investors make wise decisions with their self-directed investments. In this chapter, I will explain how a Self-Directed IRA can be used to invest in real estate notes acting as a private lender as Brant has discussed in this book. I will also cover some of the basic concepts of Self-Directed IRAs for those of you that are unfamiliar with this subject and the tremendous options available to you.

WHAT IS A SELF-DIRECTED IRA AND WHY SHOULD I HAVE ONE?

Self-Directed IRAs are a great way to take control of how you invest for retirement, but there are a lot of people who don't understand what they are or how they work. There are many misconceptions about Self-Directed IRAs and what "self-directed" really means. The truth is there really is no such thing as a Self-Directed IRA. That is just a marketing term. All IRAs are governed the same way and all IRAs have to be FDIC insured.

You may be wondering what the difference is between an IRA with a company like Charles Schwab or Fidelity and one like Quest IRA. Traditional custodians like Charles Schwab deal with publicly traded assets - like stocks, bonds, or mutual funds - and receive commission. These types of companies are licensed securities agents. At Quest IRA, we are not. We hold private assets and the assets that we hold can be any type of private asset. Most of the assets that we like to talk about at Quest relate to real estate, but there are all types of private assets that can be held. The word "self-direction" just describes the IRA. A Self-Directed IRA (SDIRA) permits the account owner to invest their IRA in what they know best, free from the investment restrictions imposed by a more traditional brokerage style account. This allows you, as the account owner, to choose from the broadest possible spectrum of investments.

Most Quest clients have an account with both us and a traditional custodian. This allows the client to participate in different investing opportunities and make the most of their retirement funds. At Quest, when cash is not invested and is just sitting in an account, there are no other options. A good system for a lot of our clients is moving money back and forth through a transfer process. They use Quest to hold their unusual assets – real estate, notes, private placements, etc. – and use a normal broker to do normal types of investing. This allows an investor the ability to get the maximum use of their money. As long as investors are transferring back and forth between two IRA custodians, they can use the transfer process and do this as many times a year, as needed.

WHAT ARE SOME OF THE BENEFITS OF A SELF-DIRECTED IRA?

DIVERSIFICATION

There are many benefits to using a self-directed IRA, but one of the biggest pros is diversification. You will hear this term a lot. Many people say it is important to diversify your portfolio. There are many different ways to diversify your portfolio, and of course, an investor could diversify it across the stock market, but they may be missing one of the biggest segments of the economy: real estate. There are many different ways to use a Self-Directed IRA to buy real estate. People use it to buy real estate directly and hold that as a rental property for long term appreciation and cash flow. They use it to buy and flip properties. They use it in the form of a bank or in lending like what the subject matter of this book is about. Sometimes they form private placements that buy larger buildings like apartment complexes with a number of passive investors providing capital to the deal. Those are all appropriate investments inside a SDIRA and they allow for true diversification. But for the purposes of this book we are going to focus on using your SDIRA to invest as a private mortgage lender, or investing in Notes is another way to say it.

TAX SAVINGS

It's also really important to understand tax savings and tax rules. IRAs are an important step and essential piece in developing wealth in a tax free way. When investing with a Self-Directed IRA, the profits made from a deal go back into the IRA and have the potential to grow tax deferred or even tax free depending on what type of account is being used. If you can learn how to use a Self-Directed IRA to invest, the tax savings can be very beneficial. As more and more IRS auditors are being hired and joining the workforce, building wealth and being an investor means understanding the tax rules and working within them to create wealth.

SOCIAL INVESTING

Another type of benefit is that of social investing. Most people are unaware of the things they invest in and the people they are invested in. If I were to ask the average American what their retirement account is invested in, they may tell me something like mutual funds or index funds, but they are unaware of the actual companies they may hold inside their retirement account. Unfortunately, in doing this (like a lot of things people use money for) they are not paying attention to where their money is and could be investing into things that do not align with their ethical or political position. With self-direction, people typically tend to be more aware of what their money is invested in because it is invested in their own backyard with local investing companies.

Here is an example of how a Self-Directed IRA can be socially beneficial. I like to lend money as a private lender like Brant has discussed in this book. And when I lend money to an investor who is using it to buy an investment property, I am able to physically drive by the property and see it. I am also able to see the repairs that are being done and the progress that is being made. I also have the peace of mind knowing the property was closed at a title company with documents prepared by a real estate attorney thus helping to secure my investment. I would also know what to do in the event the investor didn't perform and how to take the property back legally if it ever came to that situation.

In this example, I am investing in my own community and I'm helping a local real estate investor take a distressed property and fix it up to not only add value to the investment, but also to the community. By using my Self-Directed IRA to do this non-traditional investment, I am helping to create jobs by having local contractors work on the property, construction materials are being purchased from local hardware stores and the community is being revitalized. At the same time, creating a newly renovated house for a hardworking family. This is what I like to call Social Investing.

There are a lot of potentially very positive social implications when we as SDIRA investors invest in notes to help real estate investors to renovate properties. Not only do we receive above market rates of return, but the social benefits are a very nice added incentive when you're earning great returns while making your local community a better place and creating jobs in the same community where you live, work and play. This is truly rewarding experience and one of the reasons I love this type of investment personally.

INVEST IN WHAT YOU KNOW BEST

With a Self-Directed IRA, you have the opportunity to invest in things you know and understand. If you just put your money into the stock market but don't really understand what it's invested in, you may not do as well with it. Many people understand real estate and other investment pathways better than they understand mutual funds, stocks, or bonds.

If you were to invest as a SDIRA Private lender with a real estate investor that is purchasing a rental property, you could make sure there is equity in the property for starters. You could also check the borrowers background to make sure they have the ability to complete the repairs properly in order to get it rent ready for positive cash-flow. For the most part, the 'bread and butter' rental property deals are fairly straightforward. This is an example of investing in something you understand like Brant has discussed in this book. If you know about apartment complexes for example, that's what you should invest in, but single family homes are typically much easier for investors to understand.

So I will say it again, if you do not thoroughly understand an investment, self-directed or not, do not proceed! Investing in what you know best will typically yield the highest return. But always make sure you understand what to do in the worst case scenario, as well as what would happen in the best case scenario.

WHAT ARE THE DIFFERENT TYPES OF SELF-DIRECTED IRA ACCOUNTS?

There are different types of plans that can be self-directed. Like I said before, a lot of people think "self-directed" is a type of IRA, but that is not true. There are all different types of IRAs that you can invest in with your IRA. To name a few, there are personal plans, employer plans and special plans. While I won't go into detail in this book about each of these different categories, there is a tremendous amount of information about these and other SDIRA information at www.QuestIRA.com. I will also stress that it is really important to understand the types of plans and how they work because these different accounts are the tools you will use to help build your wealth completely tax free or tax-deferred.

WHAT ARE PROHIBITED TRANSACTIONS/ PEOPLE AND WHAT ARE THE CONSEQUENCES?

There are restrictions on IRAs and it's really important to understand these restrictions. Whenever we do a restricted transaction in an IRA it becomes what we call a "prohibited transaction" and it can not only effect that particular transaction but the entire IRA. You need to make sure you understand the effect and restrictions on an IRA. There are different restrictions like transaction restrictions, people restrictions and investment restrictions.

The most common restriction is a 'People Restriction'. It's important to understand there are people who are disqualified from the IRA. Those are people who can't do business with the IRA. They can't buy, sell, trade, extend services to or from, or receive a benefit, indirectly or directly from the investment the IRA makes. Those people start with you. You are a disqualified person to your IRA. You are a fiduciary to your IRA, but your IRA money isn't yours. It belongs to your IRA and doesn't belong to you again until it is distributed to you. Until then, it is held in a trust and while it is being held in that trust, you can't benefit from the investments it makes.

The benefits must be for the IRA or to make the IRA bigger. Your benefit is when you remove the money from the account in retirement.

Between you and your IRA there is a line. You can't do anything. You can't sell anything to your IRA or buy anything. If your IRA owns a house, you cannot live in that house. You cannot loan money to your IRA. You cannot advance money or extend your credit to your IRA. You must treat your IRA as an entity that is separate from you. However, you can still take your investment knowledge and skills and apply it to the IRA to help make the IRA larger, with lending to other investors and holding the notes of course.

In addition to you, there are other people who are also equally disqualified from the IRA based on the rules dealing with those who we like to call "disqualified persons." There are certain people who cannot borrow money from the IRA. The disqualified people include yourself, the IRA owner, their spouse, their lineal ascendants and descendants (children, parents, and grandparents, for example), their spouses, and any companies those people own, control, manage or are considered highly compensated by. It is important to understand that if you are going to loan money from your IRA, you can't lend it to any of those disqualified people. This would be considered a benefit to the IRA owner or someone in the family, and the IRA owner cannot benefit from loans made, whether directly or indirectly. If you can avoid that, you can do almost any type of loan.

There are also transaction restrictions and this is what the disqualified people can't do. We have already discussed this above. They can't buy, sell, trade, loan, or extend services to or from and can't benefit directly or indirectly. That is all you need to know about disqualified people for now. The transactions are just the things those people can't do.

CONSEQUENCES OF COMPLETING PROHIBITED TRANSACTIONS

The consequences of completing a prohibited transaction or doing a deal with a prohibited person can be significant. If the IRA owner gets involved in a prohibited transaction with their IRA account, the account stops being an IRA as of the first day of that year they did the investment. The account is treated as "distributing all its assets to the IRA owner at their fair market values on the first day of the year and if the total of those values is more than the basis in the IRA, the IRA owner will have a taxable gain that is included in his or her income," according to the IRS. Not only could doing a prohibited transaction close your IRA, but it could cost an investor a lot of money in taxes. The good news is these are easily avoided with a little education and proper execution and rarely an issue for the good intentioned.

HOW TO LEND IN YOUR SDIRA

You may be wondering what investments you can make with a Self-Directed IRA. Instead, you would simply ask yourself, "What investments am I knowledgeable about?" If you can take title to it, you can probably buy it in your IRA. Investment choices include: single family and multi-unit homes, tax liens, condominiums, unimproved land, foreclosures, unsecured/secured loans, limited liability companies, options, limited partnerships, joint ventures, apartments, commercial property, foreign property investments, deeds of trust and mortgages, and debt financed property. By far, Notes are the single largest asset class that we hold at Quest IRA and for good reason as they are very profitable and very predictable when done the right way as you've learned how to do in this book.

Personally, this is my preferred investment choice as a self-directed investor myself. I most often use my SDIRA to lend to real estate investors more than any other investment option and I enjoy doing it as I've previously mentioned. And while I have made a few mistakes during my many years of investing as a private lender, the overwhelming majority of my investments have been a success and even some of the ones that I had to take back ended up returning a sizeable profit as well because the deal was structured properly with a sizeable amount of equity and the proper due diligence was done on the front side.

REAL ESTATE NOTES

Mortgage notes, like mentioned earlier, are one of the most preferred ways for SDIRA investors to invest in real estate. I should also mention, that when done properly, this can be a very passive investment that can be utilized to grow your retirement account without the hassle of looking for property, renting it, maintaining it and doing a lot of the work our real estate investor borrowers have to do. A mortgage note—called a trust deed in some states—is created when one party loans money to another individual to purchase real property.

This arrangement is called private financing or of course, Private Mortgage Lending that has been covered in depth in this book.

The only difference in this way of lending is in the case of a mortgage note made from a retirement account, the payments go directly into the lender's retirement account. The terms of a mortgage note specify the type of mortgage (fixed or variable, for example), the amount of the principal, repayment schedule, and interest rate. They also obligate the borrower to repay the loan. If the borrower defaults, the lender can take the collateral. So nothing really changes when investing in notes as an SDIRA holder except the loan is made from your IRA, so the payments from the borrower will of course go to your IRA. Make sense?

Unsecured vs Secured Promissory Notes

There are two main types of notes IRAs encounter, secured notes and unsecured notes. Secured notes are backed by collateral. If the borrower fails to repay a secured note, the lender can take the collateral used to secure the note. Often, the collateral is real estate, but it can also be personal property. Unsecured notes are not backed by collateral because the lender has no simple way to be repaid if the borrower decides not to pay. This makes these investments riskier. I would never advise making an unsecured note, especially in the arena of lending to real estate investors. Please heed the advice in this book and properly secure your investments by only working with real estate investors that operate by the book with professionally prepared documents, title company closings and all of the required items Brant has suggested in this book.

STEPS TO PURCHASING AN ASSET IN A SDIRA

1. First you open an account with a third party IRA Administrator like Quest IRA and then you fund your account either by making a contribution or moving money over from an existing IRA or retirement account by completing a transfer or rollover.
2. You will locate the investment, note, etc. Remember: Quest doesn't help you find your investment. You have to do your own due diligence first.
3. Once you know what you want to invest in, you complete a few investment forms. You will need to include all required supporting documents.
4. Quest will fund the investment with your authorization. After all documents are received, Quest IRA will process the investment and send the funds to the party responsible for closing the transaction. The responsible party will close the transaction and record the deed of trust. Then, the IRA owns the mortgage or secured note.

PARTNERING IRAS

Although there are rules put in place for disqualified people, you are able to partner IRAs together. Often, if you are looking to form or put together a loan, you might look at your budget and see that you can partner a couple of IRAs together to reach this monetary goal.

For example, your Traditional IRA has money, and maybe your spouse's IRA also has some money. You notice you also have personal money, and maybe even some money in another type of savings account, like a HSA. It is true that all of those are disqualified persons to each other and can't do business with each other, meaning they can't buy, sell, trade, or extend services to or from one another, but whether or not you are buying or lending money, you must understand that it doesn't prohibit you from partnering those together.

You can take an IRA, like a traditional IRA and a Roth IRA, and use them to do an investment together. You divide it up by the percentages of ownership. For example, you can make it Quest IRA FBO John Doe's IRA #12345 as to an undivided interest of 60% and to John Doe's Roth #67891 as to an undivided interest of 40%. The percentages are up to you and can be anything. As long as the income and the expenses related to the investment can be split exactly according to the percentages of ownership, partnering is absolutely allowed and I would even say is encouraged.

If you look at most people's households, you will find they have a lot of different types of retirement accounts throughout their household. They might also have varying types of money. The ability to pick up all those different types of accounts, put them together, and use one piece of leverage is important whether you are the lender or the borrower. You don't necessarily have to understand all the types of accounts; you just have to know that they can work together. It is a good idea when you are putting these accounts together to ask an

IRA Specialist to help you understand the unique roles the different IRAs play. You can always call Quest, and a specialist can help you better understand how to partner IRAs together to create a note.

Chapter Takeaways

There are many benefits to using a self-directed IRA as part of your investment strategy and this can be a valuable tool in your journey as a private mortgage lender and one of the greatest ways to grow your wealth. The key to using this investment vehicle wisely is understanding what it is, how it benefits you as an investor, and what your options are for opening and utilizing your account(s).

In order to make the most of your IRA as a lending tool, you need to first understand the ins and outs of investing with an IRA as well as how to protect yourself. Once you understand what a self-directed IRA is and how to properly utilize it into your investment strategy, you will be able to make more informed decisions to maximize your wealth and live more comfortably in retirement. Learning the basics of this now will open up new opportunities for you later as you continue to invest and build further wealth.

Be sure to visit the
Private Lender Playbook page
to access valuable tools & resources

www.PrivateLenderPlaybook.com

Chapter 13: Nathan's Rules

"As time goes on, I get more and more convinced that the right method of investment is to put fairly large sums into enterprises which one thinks one knows something about and in the management of which one thoroughly believes."

– J.M. Keynes

The following chapter was contributed by Nathan Long, CEO of Quest IRA.

I would like to start this chapter by sharing that I have personally had to foreclose several times throughout my lending career. I know this is the number one fear of many private lenders and many of my self-directed IRA clients. And I will also tell you that every single time I ended up doing a foreclosure, the net return was higher than if I would have just received my interest back. The reason is I have developed and followed a personal set of rules for lending that have helped keep me on the straight and narrow and enabled me to make the right decision when determining if I should lend to someone. I want to share these rules with you as well as some of my lending experiences that I hope will help you make smarter decisions in your own investment journey.

RULE #1: DON'T INVEST IN SOMETHING YOU WOULDN'T BE EXCITED TO OWN IF THE BORROWER DEFAULTS

In the event of default, you need to understand two things:

1. What is the procedure for collecting on the debt in the event of default? And again, if you are dealing with real estate, the procedure is usually a foreclosure, and that process is much easier than if you were secured by some other type of asset.
2. What do you do with that asset once you obtain it? For example, what are you going to do if you loan to a borrower who purchases 10 tons of copper wire? There is not much you can do with that.

When I am loaning money I like to stick to real estate because the foreclosure process makes it easy in the event of default. Also, I like to loan money on things I know and understand. Personally, I don't go for high, expensive homes because sometimes those can be hard to get rid of, but I also don't like to loan in areas that are too inexpensive either. I like medium priced homes because I know what to do with those. I would suggest not loaning on something you are not prepared to take over or do something with should the borrower default and lastly, if the thought of taking the collateral back doesn't truly excite you, then you may want to keep your eyes open for another opportunity.

RULE #2: DON'T ADVANCE FUNDS FOR REPAIRS UNTIL THEY ARE COMPLETE

I get in trouble with some of my borrowers with this second rule, so I want to explain. Generally, I don't advance funds for repairs until the repairs are done. I also inspect before advancing.

For example, many times I will have a borrower come to me and say, "I can buy this house for $50,000. There is $20,000 worth of repairs needed for the property. When I get it all done, it's going to be worth $100,000." That is a pretty good position for me as a lender. I am at a 70% loan to value ratio. I will be on the first lien on that loan, so this deal makes a lot of sense to me.

In this case, I would let the borrower know I will give him the whole $70,000 that he needs to purchase the property, to close, and to do the repairs. However, at the time of closing, I am only going to release a portion of the allocated money for repairs. This may be $5,000 for example, or just enough for the borrower to complete the first set of repairs. After they are finished with the first set of repairs, I will come out, inspect, and fund that set of completed repairs. Once this is done, we can move on to the second set round of repairs and inspections. I include my escrow sheet, which I usually have my attorney draft into the note so I know this information is there. We do this because we don't want to just hand the investor $20,000 at closing. The investor could just take the money and run, or if they don't do the repairs correctly, it could cause the lender to become responsible.

With that being said, when the investor calls and says all the repairs are completed, it is important that you immediately inspect and get a check cut to your borrower. If you are funding from an IRA at Quest, it's an easy process. Our Accounts Payable Department cuts checks very quickly. You can usually get a check within 24 hours.

Though I believe it is good to hold back on the repair fund, there are times when I break this rule. For example, I had one investor that I knew well and had done many deals with. They bought a property costing around $20,000, but the repairs were almost $60,000. It was a very heavy rehab that required an almost complete rebuild of the home. In this case, I knew there was a lot of equity in the property itself. It was worth a lot more than just the $20,000. In this case, I loaned the borrower $20,000 to purchase the property and advanced another $20,000 for repairs at closing.

Why did I do it in advance of any repairs being done? There are a couple of reasons. I felt like I was always secured. There was always enough equity in the property itself. Also, I have done business with this person for a long time, and I knew he always did a great job with rehabs, so there was a certain level of trust. In addition, a lot of the deal was dependent on the repairs. I think it would have been very difficult for the investor to make that particular deal without some type of advancement of funds to be used for the renovations.

This is not a rule that I break often, but when it makes sense for the deal, I do take time to consider. When we talk about private money lending, whether you are the lender or the borrower, it is always a private negotiation. We always need to look at what makes sense for all parties involved.

RULE #3: DO NOT LOAN TO SOMEONE YOU WOULD FEEL UNCOMFORTABLE FORECLOSING ON

You should not loan to anyone that you would feel uncomfortable foreclosing on. The disqualified persons list is very specific for self-directed IRAs. You cannot loan to your spouse, your lineal ascendants or descendants, their spouses, or companies any of those people own, control, manage, or are highly compensated by. A girlfriend or boyfriend is not on that list, but I have seen many instances where loaning to someone you love can create a lot of drama.

When you are talking about loaning money from an IRA, it should be a business transaction. The people that you loan to should be people that are not related to you since this is a business transaction, so in the event of default you will not feel bad foreclosing on them. If you loan to a girlfriend or boyfriend and something goes wrong with that deal, unfortunately when it hits your IRA you are going to have to make an attempt to collect it or have to pay taxes on that full amount to remove it from the IRA. In this situation, you would have to hire an attorney to go after your significant other in order to correct it within the IRA.

I have also seen other issues arise with lending to loved ones. A man lent money to his girlfriend who is not a disqualified person. The IRS came back and said that he still did a prohibited transaction. The IRS could see that his girlfriend was very close to him, and they could see that the two shared a home, assets, and even a checking account together. When he loaned money to his girlfriend, it is true she received a benefit, but he also received an indirect benefit because it went into a checking account held by the both of them. Therefore, the IRS deemed it a prohibited transaction, not because he loaned money to his girlfriend, but rather because he also received a personal benefit from that loan. Always be careful when loaning money to someone you would feel uncomfortable foreclosing on or in any situation that may be considered a prohibited transaction.

RULE #4: TAKE IMMEDIATE ACTION WHEN THE LOAN GOES INTO DEFAULT

If the loan goes into default, do not delay. By the time that you are 20-days past due, you should have contacted a qualified real estate attorney, and they should be waiting there with the letter to show the default. This will let your borrowers know that you are serious and that they need to pay you immediately.

The worst thing you can do is not take action. I have seen people loan money out and not receive payments for five years! Going through a foreclosure can sometimes be complicated if you have not done it before, but trust me when I say you will feel much better about taking action rather than letting it go into default. It will also set your level of expectation immediately, meaning if it happens once with your borrower, it will most likely never happen again.

RULE #5: COLLECT INTEREST MONTHLY

This is another rule that sometimes gets me in trouble with borrowers. I always collect monthly interest, and the reason I do this isn't necessarily just to have cash flow. I collect monthly interest so that in the event something goes wrong, I am able to collect.

For example, say I do a one-year loan for my borrower and my borrower passes on, becomes unhealthy, or can't finish the deal for some reason, but he has made regular payments. He isn't in default, and he hasn't failed to make a payment to me; he just isn't available for whatever reason. I would have to wait until the end of the year and allow my house to sit that entire period of time before I could foreclose.

Requiring monthly interest payment allows me to have a trigger to go in and start the foreclosure process. I know that borrowers don't like this because when they are doing a flip, they don't get paid until the end. There are a few things for borrowers to consider though. First of all, I think borrowers would have a better time borrowing from IRAs if they paid a monthly interest. A lot of the people using IRA money to lend are actually creating cash flow with which they can live on. They already have several thousands of dollars in retirement, so they want to create cash flow without disrupting their principle. Loans work very well for that.

When borrowers pay interest in a lump sum at the end, it can make them unattractive to a lot of lenders. It is also just the cost of money, and you should be calculating the cost of your money as part of your deal. Right from the beginning this should be something that goes into your calculation and it should be something you think about as you go through the transactions and the process of the deal. I always recommend collecting interest and designing your notes the way I have described just in case something happens.

RULE #6: CONSULT WITH THE EXPERTS

If you are unsure about a loan, always hire someone to help you. You should get a second opinion on every single loan you participate in. You always want to make sure the loan is reasonable and structured properly.

This doesn't always have to be an attorney. You could hire a real estate coach, like Brant, to look at the deal and help you better understand the property. You could even hire a realtor to get a realtor's opinion of value. Again, I would recommend having a brief conversation with the attorney that is drafting the documents and to make sure they are a lenders attorney and advising on your behalf.

RULE #7: ALWAYS MAKE SURE THE BORROWER GETS TITLE INSURANCE AND CLOSES AT THE TITLE COMPANY

I know this is something Brant covered in an earlier chapter, but it is so important that I'd like to reiterate it here. Table-top closings just aren't wise. The number one thing that ruins real estate deals is the chain of title. All types of things can create chain of title problems, even if no one has done anything wrong. That's why it's important to clean the chain of title. Doing so includes closing at a title company and getting title insurance on that loan.

There is one other thing I require, and it is called a mortgagee clause. In other words, not only is there title insurance for the borrower in the event that there is a title problem, but in the event that I have to foreclose, that title insurance will cover me as the lender as well. Title insurance companies are a very important part of the real estate process, and I think you should always close at a title company and get mortgage insurance on the loan.

RULE #8: ALWAYS VERIFY HAZARD AND FLOOD INSURANCE AND INSIST ON EVIDENCE THAT PROPERTY TAXES ARE PAID WHENEVER THEY BECOME DUE

If the lender and borrower close at a title company, most of the time the title company is going to collect fees. Often when I am loaning money, there are occasions when the borrower might need an extension. I don't mind doing an extension if the property is still secured, and I am getting the rate of return I was expecting. I always insist they show proof they have paid the insurance and the taxes. Then I verify they have paid them myself. I will typically call the borrower or get online to see that the property taxes have been paid. This is very important, because property taxes supersede your lien. Also, if your house burns down and you have no insurance, your lien isn't going to be worth very much.

In addition to that, you need to double check the hazard insurance at the time of closing to verify that you are listed as a lender. If it is your IRA, you need to have the complete vesting of your IRA listed as the lender. It should look like this: Quest IRA, Inc. FBO [your name] IRA [account number].

RULE #9: ALWAYS MAKE SURE TO GET A PERSONAL GUARANTEE IF YOU'RE LENDING TO AN ENTITY

Truthfully, I prefer lending to an entity. Most real estate investors form an entity when they are buying real estate. The purpose of this is to isolate lawsuits, but we don't want them isolating themselves against the lender. They are supposed to be guaranteeing the lender, so that is why I always ask for a personal guarantee. In the event of a default which has occurred because someone has died, it may be easier to avoid probate if there is an entity in there that is the lender instead of the individual themselves. I always try to ask my borrowers to form an LLC before lending to them for that reason.

RULE #10: TRY TO BE IN THE FIRST LIEN POSITION

Typically when I am lending from an IRA, I want to be in first lien position. If I am in a second lien position – at least here in Texas – the first lien position could wipe out my second lien in the event of default. Furthermore, in the second lien position, I would have the opportunity to pay off the first lien and take over the entire property, but if I don't have enough money in my IRA to pay off the first lien, then the opportunity to pay it off wouldn't do me much good. I would avoid most 2nd lien opportunities in most cases and focus more on first lien opportunities, if possible.

RULES FOR THE BORROWER

In addition to the rules I've provided above that I follow as a lender, I've also included some general rules for borrowers who are investing in real estate.

OPI: OTHER PEOPLE'S IRA'S

Using other people's money is a way to create your own private funding source. A lot of people have a funny concept about borrowing money. It almost feels like they think they are a beggar. I can tell you from being a lender, whenever I lend money, it's very relieving. It is out on the market, and I am earning money so I feel very good about the money that is out there. The first thing a borrower needs to do is get out of their head that they are begging.

The next thing to understand is that whenever you are engaging in private money deals, it's a relationship building process. Lenders may be very wary of you at the beginning, but that is only because they have not had time to build a relationship with you. Most of the time you don't need hundreds of private lenders to do hundreds of real estate transactions. You only need a few private lenders who trust you and that you develop a relationship with.

Here's an example. When I'm lending, typically I will partner my IRAs with other members of my family like my brother or cousin, as this allows us to pool our money together to make a complete loan to the borrower. When I last looked at my records, I realized I had sixteen different loans out to one borrower. He continues to borrow money and bring me great deals, and I am very comfortable with him. I didn't intend to give out 16 loans to him, but it worked very well for the borrower and myself because we developed a relationship over the years.

Make sure you're taking time not just to borrow the money, but to make a relationship with your lender. If you develop a good relationship, this lender will most likely continue to let you borrow money and refer you to other people in their household for years to come. Remember, when you talk to people, they may have different types of buckets of money. Also, using multiple types of accounts like Traditional funds, Roth funds, SEP funds, etc., can increase the amount of money you can borrow.

THINGS TO CONSIDER IF YOU WANT TO BORROW MONEY

Here are some things you should consider if you want to borrow money from a private lender for your next real estate deal:

1. BUILD AND FOSTER YOUR RELATIONSHIP WITH THE LENDER

Borrowing private money really is all about one thing: your relationship with the lender. Every time I go out and give a speech, usually 300 times a year, I'll have someone run up to me, throw their hands up, and say, "I have $250,000!" I'll sigh and think to myself, "I don't even know this person, or the deal." I think this is common for a lot of people. I like to think of it like dating. Imagine you were at a bar or social event and you just walked up to the first person you saw and blurted out everything on your mind. I think this might cause you to run into some problems. Instead, try engaging yourself in some polite conversation. Maybe try to be funny and tell some jokes. If you feel comfortable, maybe you can get a phone number and see if that leads to texting or even going on a date. Eventually you can approach the bigger subject that you wanted to talk about. Well, this is what it is like developing a relationship, and I think borrowing private money should start the same way. You want to start by building the relationship.

Try to take the lender's temperature when it comes to their risk tolerance and how eager they are for the income. You need to understand what their needs are and match your programs to their needs. I once had a person who was borrowing money from an investor, and this particular investment was very tight. They didn't have a lot of extra money and they had loaned every little bit of money they had to the investor. Sure enough, after they started the rehab, the borrower had an emergency and they needed money right away. It was a big hassle for the borrower to meet the lender's needs. In that case, it would be beneficial to hold back some money for emergencies.

Maybe they desire to have a certain amount of money free each month, so it would be important to design a loan so that amount is achieved. Pay attention to the lender and their needs while you work to develop that relationship. You also want to try to take care of them by understanding the foreclosure process, having the proper attorney, and making the payments on time…every single time.

2. MAKE THE PROCESS PAINLESS FOR YOUR LENDER

If done with an IRA, sometimes the lending process can be complex. At Quest, we try to make it as simple as possible, but dealing with the IRS, the government, and banks can still be very difficult. There is a lot of paperwork like transfer forms and account opening forms, and the forms range from being very easy to being extremely complicated. There is also paperwork when getting the loan documents drafted.

It is very important for the borrower to understand the process, and if you don't, make sure you ask questions so you can be there for your lender when they have the same questions. You want to hold their hand through the process so they feel comfortable and make it is as simple for them as possible. The lender should only have to sign the paperwork the borrower and their attorney prepare. The lender shouldn't have to do much more than lend the money.

3. MAKE SURE TO PROTECT THE LENDER'S INTEREST AT ALL TIMES

Your reputation is ten times more important than anything else if you are a private borrower. If you take care of your lender, even if you are losing money on the deal, they will probably take care of you for the rest of your investing career as they continue to fund many other transactions. However, as soon as you don't pay your lender or you pay them late, it will get out in the community which could cause you to lose a lot of opportunities for borrowing.

4. Don't approach a lender until you have all the information.

Provide the lender with the details of the transaction, including your price and comparable sales to show value. You will need to have all of the information ready. Knowing the exit strategy, what you plan on doing with the property, and knowing why it is a good deal is extremely important. Never "fluff" the deal. If you have to exaggerate the deal to make it look appealing to the lender, you probably don't have a good enough deal, and you may need to go back and rework the numbers until it looks right. Always make sure you have a clear perspective of the deal.

5. Have a portfolio of successful deals

Be sure to carry a success book. This is not necessary, but it always helps if lenders want to see examples of your past deals. Include pictures showcasing what the house looked like before and after. This success book or deal portfolio will really help you gain credibility by showing some of the successful projects you have already done.

Chapter Takeaways

I have developed the rules above through my own personal experiences as an investor. Though you don't have to follow my rules, they can help save you time and hassle when becoming a private money lender. Consider each of them carefully as you start to build your own set of rules. Remember, sometimes rules are meant to be broken and you need to consider what works best for each individual deal.

When considering potential borrowers, look for those that follow some of my borrower rules. These factors can be the difference between an okay borrower that you work with on one deal and a great borrower that can continue to help you meet your investing goals for years to come.

Chapter 14: Foreclosure

"Rule No.1: Never lose money. Rule No.2: Never forget rule No.1."

– Warren Buffett

I will start this chapter by once again reminding everyone that I am not an attorney, nor have I ever personally dealt with a foreclosure, other than buying them as investment properties. But I do want to address the topic of foreclosure very briefly. Personally, I have successfully invested in hundreds of deals and have never faced anything near a foreclosure. Nor have I ever been late in making a payment, other than the occasional admin or auto-bill pay error. I assure you I'm not mentioning this to brag or impress anyone, but rather to impress upon you the fact that there are hundreds, if not thousands of other companies and real estate investors like myself that operate very successful businesses all over the country who navigate through the market for years and even decades without ever creating a foreclosure situation. My encouragement is for you to consider Benjamin Franklin's advice; "an ounce of prevention is worth a pound of cure". Be sure to perform the proper due diligence before proceeding on any deal so you can prevent a foreclosure situation to ever occur. Additionally, I think it's also worth noting since I began private lending myself over five years ago, I have never had to foreclose on any of my borrowers.

All of that being said, I understand that as a lender, it is normal to be concerned about the possibility of foreclosure. In most lender's minds, they see foreclosures as the worst case scenario. While it is understandable to have this viewpoint, this bad ending could have resulted from a deal that wasn't structured properly on the front end and the fact that there is not enough equity in the property.

However, I want to reinforce an insight that we've discussed before. While it may still seem counterintuitive to most fledgling lenders, when your deals are structured properly, you can make greater returns in the event of a foreclosure. I know this was alluded to earlier in the book, but I do want to touch on it again. Just think about it, it's really simple math. As a real estate investor, when we flip houses, our typical profits are in the $25,000 - $40,000 range. Many of our deals exceed $50,000 in profit and some exceed the $100,000 mark! When you are lending, you are typically earning 7 - 10% interest, which isn't bad. But if you invested into a deal that has equity in the $30,000 to $50,000 range, and if you have to take the property back, guess who would own that equity? Yep, that would be you my friend.

For private lenders who structure their deals properly with adequate amounts of equity, foreclosure is not always a worst case scenario situation. It could often turn out to be the best case scenario for you financially, provided you have done your lending correctly. I understand that a foreclosure is likely something you never want to deal with. But, it is nice to have the peace of mind if it ever came to a foreclosure situation, that because you structured things correctly, and analyzed the deal thoroughly, your work and effort would pay off.

While I don't think it is necessary to have an in-depth understanding of the foreclosure process, I do think it is imperative to have a baseline of knowledge and know who to call in the event you are faced with a possible foreclosure situation. So what takes place in the event you do need to initiate a foreclosure? I will first say the foreclosure process varies greatly from state to state, but since I'm a Texas resident and investor, I will share what I know about the foreclosure process here in Texas. Keep in mind the foreclosure process is based on the state the property is located in, not in the state where the borrower or the lender resides.

FORECLOSURE PROCESS

Here are the four basic steps to the foreclosure process in Texas:

Step 1: Send a notice of default and demand to cure default at earliest allowable moment per the loan documents. It is common to send a 20-day notice.

Step 2: Send notice of acceleration and copy of foreclosure posting at least 21 days prior to foreclosure.

Step 3: Post foreclosure notice on a notice board at county courthouse, and file the original notice in the real property records where the property is located.

Step 4: Foreclose on the first Tuesday of every month.

In Texas, it is extremely easy for lenders to go through the foreclosure process. It starts with your attorney sending a notice of default to the borrower. Typically, the borrower needs to be 20-days late with their payment. Once the borrower receives the 20-day notice, your attorney will send a notice of acceleration and a copy of the foreclosure posting at least 21 days prior to the foreclosure. A foreclosure notice will need to be posted on the notice board at the county courthouse and it will also need to be filed in the real property records. I want to point out it is strongly suggested that you hire a qualified real estate attorney to handle the foreclosure process and not perform these actions on your own. From what I've heard, this is not a very expensive process.

Lastly, you actually complete the foreclosure process. Every county in Texas forecloses on the first Tuesday of each month. If you're paying attention to the timeline, depending on when the first Tuesday of the month occurs, you can foreclose in the state of Texas in less than 41 days. This type of foreclosure has no redemption rights, meaning the homeowner has no right to 'redeem' their property after the foreclosure is complete. About half of the states have laws that give homeowners the ability to redeem their property for a period of time after the foreclosure sale, however, Texas is not one of those states. So at this point, there is essentially no going back, and you own the property.

Foreclosure can be an extremely easy process in our state and many others, but certainly more complex and timely in some states. One thing you may want to research beforehand is if you live in a judicial or nonjudicial foreclosure state. In a judicial foreclosure state, the lender has to file a lawsuit in court in order to foreclose, which of course will likely be more time consuming and more expensive. Nonjudicial foreclosure states allow the lender to foreclose without going through the court system. Some states, like Texas, provide the ability for either option. I know this is a deciding factor for some lenders, and they prefer to invest in states like Texas in the event they have to foreclose on a borrower.

There are many more aspects and intricacies of the foreclosure process and each state is different. This is certainly not my area of expertise, therefore that is as far as we are going to go on this subject. I encourage you to do some research on your own and possibly consider speaking to a local real estate attorney about the foreclosure process in your state to gain some insight to how the foreclosure process is handled. It helps to be an educated lender, but hopefully this is something you will never have to face. My intention in this chapter was to give you a very basic introduction to this topic and provide a few pointers to help steer you in the right direction in the event you're ever faced with this situation. I hope I have helped accomplish that goal.

Chapter Takeaways

Though most investors see foreclosure as the worst-case scenario, there are many times when foreclosure can actually work in the investor's favor. If you want the foreclosure process to go smoothly, it is vital that you do your due diligence up-front. Be sure that you have a solid set of loan documents, prepared by a trusted real estate attorney, as well as an adequate amount of equity in the property in the event you have to foreclose. Make sure that you understand the foreclosure process and any loan documentation regarding foreclosure before you sign any loan agreements.

To better understand the foreclosure process in the state (or states) where you plan to invest, be sure to do your research and consult with a real estate attorney before you enter into any investments. Learning about the foreclosure process before you even begin investing will help you avoid any issues later down the road should you need to foreclose on a property.

Chapter 15: Case Studies

"Things may come to those who wait, but only the things left by those who hustle."

— *Abraham Lincoln*

Now that you understand the basics of private mortgage lending and how to structure your loans, you might be wondering what this all looks like in the real world. It is one thing to discuss potential loan terms and talk about what you might make on a deal, and it is quite another to see it in action. I think one of the best ways to show new private mortgage lenders how their money can work for them over time is to look at some examples of actual deals.

Therefore I've put together a couple of case studies of recent deals that my company has invested in with the backing of our private lenders investment capital. These example deals will help you better understand what private loans can look like on short and long-term deals and illustrate the value private mortgage lending can provide when it comes to investing. In this chapter, I'll discuss two different properties – a flip and a rental – and explain the breakdown of each private loan so you can better understand how you may be able to put your own money to work for you in similar deals.

CASE STUDY #1: FLIP

This flip property, located on a street called La Entrada, is a single-family mostly brick home, approximately 1,500 square feet with three bedrooms, two bathrooms, and a two-car garage. For our company, this is the ideal home for a flip project or even rental property for that matter. Our team found the property through a motivated seller who responded to one of our marketing pieces we send out every month through mailers and other marketing campaigns. The home had a purchase price of $96,000 and after taking a look at the property, we allotted $19,000 for repairs. This brought our total loan amount to $115,000. Our property analysis determined the home's ARV to be approximately $159,000.

For this deal, we received a $115,000 loan from a private lender's self-directed IRA our company has been working with for a very long time. Typically, for flip properties, this private lender makes loans to us in exchange for a 10% interest return, and that is what they offered us on this loan. The private lender also earned a 1% or 1 point origination fee, which came to $1,150 on this deal. This fee was paid at closing when we purchased the property.

The loan was a 12-month loan and the payment terms included accrued interest. This means we did not make monthly payments to the lender. Instead, the loan accrued interest until the sale of the property. In most lending transactions, lenders will collect monthly interest on their loans. However, many of our lenders make loans to us with accrued interest and this tends to be more from our SDIRA lenders than cash lenders. In this case study, a $115,000 investment at 10% interest, would come out to monthly payments, or in this instance, interest accrual of $958.33 every month. It is important to note we never create loan guidelines with accrued interest on rental properties, which are long-term investments with longer timelines.

Overall, the private lender's loan to value (LTV) was 72%. This falls within the standard range for an acceptable LTV on a flip deal of 70 to 75%. After the repairs were completed, the property was listed and sold for our anticipated price of $159,000. With a total loan length of 94 days from start to finish, the private lender had a return on their investment (ROI) of $4,111.64. This came to about a 15% rate of return.

To get a bigger picture view of this deal, here is the loan information as described above:

- Property Type: Single-Family Home
- Investment Strategy: Flip
- Loan Amount: $115,000
- Purchase Price: $96,000
- Repairs: $19,000
- Value of Property (ARV): $159,000
- Loan To Value: 72%
- Interest Rate: 10%
- Points: 1 pt.
- Term: 12 months
- Payment Terms: Accrued Interest
- Total Length of Loan: 94 days
- Return on Investment in 94 days: $4,111.64
- Rate of Return: 15%

This deal is a great example of a typical flip property investment. The case study illustrates what private mortgage lenders can stand to profit from in short-term flip deals like this. If you would like to see this property, you can go to www.PrivateLenderPlaybook.com and look for the link to case study videos. There you will find some before and after images from the repairs and renovations our team at Invest Home Pro made on the property and many other videos.

CASE STUDY #2: RENTAL

The second example I'm going to discuss is a long-term rental property investment, on a street named Hollow Wood. This is a single-family home we purchased to be used as rental property. We found this property through a wholesaler, who brings our company deals for an agreed upon transaction fee. The purchase price was $75,000 and we allotted $25,000 for repairs. This brought the total loan amount to $100,000, which we borrowed from a private mortgage lender. The interest rate on this private loan was 8% with a 1 point origination fee, which means the lender received $1,000 at the purchase closing.

The loan term for this rental property was 60 months (five years). Although we never had the intention of keeping the investor's money invested in this property for that long, this was the term that we agreed upon. Let me explain. Typically, we will structure rental property loans for two to five years even though we do not necessarily plan on keeping the money for the entire period of time. We structure the loan in this way to provide some security just in case there are any major shifts in the market or any issues that may arise when it comes time to refinance the loan with our long-term lenders/banks. The intention with this deal was to purchase the property and hold it for one or two years before beginning to refinance the loan at a lower interest rate with the bank while still giving our lender a nice return for an extended period of time. And in some instances, when lenders are happy earning 5 - 7%, we absolutely will keep the money invested in the property for up 5 years and sometimes even longer.

Typically, for rental properties the LTV is around the 75% mark, however for rental properties, there are some exceptions to the rule that will justify going slightly over the 75% mark if other factors support this decision. For this deal, the lender's LTV came to 77%, which was still a remarkable deal for the type of property we bought in a market with solid appreciation. When it comes to payment terms, we agreed to make monthly payments of $667. The terms included a 20-year amortization with a 5-year balloon. This means the loan was not an interest only loan, but rather amortized over 20 years so each month our payments were reducing the amount of principal owed on the property. The loan terms required this investment be paid off or refinanced within the 5-year period of time. Amortizing loans reduces the amount of invested capital our lenders have in the deal each and every month after a payment is made. Typically, private lender loans are simple interest only loans, but we prefer to amortize our rental property loans with our lenders, but not always. This is something you will need to discuss with your borrower and outline in depth in the loan documents prior to closing.

After the property was renovated, we leased it for $1,275 per month. The property value at the time was approximately $130,000 after repairs and renovations. The total length of the loan for which we kept the investor's money working for them was 665 days before refinancing this loan. The return on investment for the private money lender came to $16,033.14 with an 8.45% rate of return. This rate of return factors in the 1-point origination fee that was paid at closing at the original purchase.

Again, here's a bigger picture view of this deal with the loan information as described above:

- Property Type: Single-Family Home
- Investment Strategy: Rental
- Loan Amount: $100,000
- Purchase Price: $75,000
- Repairs: $25,000
- Value of Property (ARV): $130,000
- Loan To Value: 77%
- Interest Rate: 8%
- Points: 1 pt.
- Term: 60 months
- Payment Terms: $677 monthly
- Payment Terms: 20 Year Amortization / 5 Year Balloon
- Total Length of Loan: 665 days
- Return on Investment in 94 days: $16,033.14
- Rate of Return: 8.45%

This case study of a typical rental deal shows you just how you can make your money work for you over time when lending on long-term rental properties. Though the interest rate in our rental case study example was lower than the flip property, the loan term was longer meaning the private mortgage lender stands to gain more as their money works for them over a longer period of time without a stagnant period of time not earning interest. And, by the way, we did refinance this property with one of our bank lenders in a little less than 24 months, so our private lender received all of their capital back and reinvested it with us again on a new deal shortly thereafter.

Again, if you want to see more about this property and take a look at the home before and after the repairs and renovations, visit www.PrivateLenderPlaybook.com and look for the link to case studies.

Chapter Takeaways

These case studies are great examples of typical flip and rental deals showing just what private mortgage lenders stand to gain when they make their money work for them in the real estate market. Hopefully, these real-world examples of private mortgage loans give you a better idea of how these loans can be structured, what the numbers may look like and what private lenders can earn over time when engaging in these types of deals.

In an earlier chapter, we discussed the difference between short-term and long-term investments. When comparing these two examples of deals, you can see the difference in value between flip properties (short-term investments), especially at higher interest rates, and rental properties (long-term investments). Remember, it is important to consider what your investment goals are as well as other items such as liquidity, risk tolerance, and other circumstances before you start looking for potential deals. But to each their own and I'm confident you will determine the best investing strategy to meet your personal financial goals.

Be sure to visit the
Private Lender Playbook page
to access valuable tools & resources

www.PrivateLenderPlaybook.com

Chapter 16: Frequently Asked Questions (FAQs)

I get a lot of questions from new and aspiring private lenders about the process and technicalities of private mortgage lending. Though I've tried to answer most of these questions in this book, there may be a few that I haven't gotten to yet. That's why I have put together a list of questions that I get asked most often by new private mortgage lenders. Feel free to refer to this list as you start your journey into private lending.

IS THERE A MINIMUM INVESTMENT FOR PRIVATE LENDERS?

Technically, there is no minimum investment private lenders are required to have in order to invest in a real estate project. I have worked with lenders with just $10,000 and up to $2,000,000 when they first get started. Everyone has to start somewhere. Typically, private mortgage lenders start out in the $100,000 to $300,000 range. If you are starting off with less to lend, there is a good chance there is an investor out there who needs a smaller loan amount like the one you are able to offer.

On the flip side, some private mortgage lenders have their own minimum investment. For example, a lender might not offer loan amounts to investors less than $150,000. This is a personal decision based on the lender's own preferences.

Many private lenders may not find it worthwhile to participate in loans that are less than a certain amount.

CAN I LIQUIDATE A LOAN?

Technically, you can liquidate a loan, or make the private loan liquid to get your funds back, but only if that is something expressly written in the loan note and if the real estate investor has that money available. For instance, what I make available sometimes to certain clients is a 90-day due on demand clause that allows them to call the loan due at basically any time, but it gives me 90 days to pay off the loan or find another lender to refinance. That's about the only way a private lender can liquidate a private loan without having to discount the note and sell it to another investor.

It is important to note that if you anticipate you will need to make the private loan liquid in the near future, then private mortgage lending is not the best investment outlet for you at that time. I really don't recommend anyone lending money if they see any chance of them needing their money back before the loan term is complete. To avoid this situation entirely, make sure you understand your personal financial situation and investment goals clearly before lending, and don't lend more capital than you can spare.

HOW DO I MAKE SURE THE TAXES AND INSURANCE ARE PAID ON A PROPERTY?

It is important that any properties you have loaned money on are up-to-date with both the taxes and insurance. To make sure the taxes have been paid on a property, you will need to check with the county and/or taxing entity the property is located in each year. To make sure you do this, I suggest adding a reminder as a task to your annual calendar.

As for insurance, if you have structured your loan agreement as discussed earlier, you should be named as the additional insured on the property. That means if anything changes – if the borrower makes a change to the insurance coverage or stops paying the insurance – you will get an immediate notification. However, I also recommend you check in with the insurance company every 90-days. Rather than asking the borrower, email the insurance company directly to make sure the property is still properly insured. This is a simple and quick procedure, but the peace of mind is invaluable.

WHAT COSTS DO PRIVATE MONEY LENDERS INCUR?

It is fairly standard for the borrower to pay for all of the fees involved with the closing process, including loan documentation, preparations, attorneys, etc. I recommend all private mortgage lenders request these fees be paid by the borrower as this is the standard way of doing business. In fact, there are only two potential fees we don't pay when borrowing from a private lender, and those are for appraisals/ BPOs or attorney review fees.

We provide a fairly in-depth valuation of the property from our full-time real estate agent, so we don't provide or pay for appraisals or BPOs. Our lenders are welcome to order them any time to confirm our assessments, but they would do so at their own expense. Additionally, while we pay for all of the attorney's fees, document preparation and closing costs, occasionally a lender will want their personal attorney to review the paperwork, which I completely understand, however, this would be done at the lenders expense and not typically paid by to the borrower.

It's also important to mention the private lender would also incur fees in the event of a foreclosure. If the home goes into foreclosure, then the lender will need to pay various foreclosure fees. However, many promissory notes include fees that are incurred due to foreclosure would be added to the balance of the debt.

WHAT IS A PERSONAL GUARANTEE?

A personal guarantee is when the borrower provides a guarantee to the private lender for the outstanding loan amount in addition to any legal fees, accrued interest, and costs associated with debt collection. This guarantee allows the lender to look to the borrower's personal assets when recovering any unpaid balance that is not satisfied by property foreclosure and resale. There are a few different types of personal guarantees including limited personal guarantees, which set a limit on the amount of liability, and conditional personal guarantees, which require a specific event to trigger the guarantee.

WHAT ARE POINTS, AND DO PMLS HAVE TO REQUIRE THEM?

Points are finance charges on the private loan typically paid at loan closing. Each point equals 1% of the total loan amount. For example, if you ask for 2 points on a $100,000 loan, then the points would equal $2,000. Some private lenders choose not to charge points, while others may ask for a flat fee instead of a percentage.

There is no right or wrong answer when it comes to charging points. Some lenders charge 1, 2, 3 and sometimes even 4 points and some lenders don't charge at all. You just have to be cautious when deciding whether to charge points. If you become too aggressive with these fees then you may miss out on some potential deals as it can cause borrowers to look elsewhere for a private loan.

DO PRIVATE MORTGAGE LOANS ONLY SERVE RISKY OR DESPERATE BORROWERS?

Not at all. It's a common misconception that private mortgage loans are only for those real estate investors who cannot get a loan from the bank. I've illustrated throughout this book the many benefits of private lending when you have properly analyzed the deal and the borrower. Real estate investors work with private lenders because there is a definite need for them in the marketplace. Private lender loans allow real estate investors to fund their deals quickly and with less documentation they may otherwise have lost if they were dependent upon the banks. In fact, many real estate investors will work with both private lenders and banks to get the funds they need for their investments.

HOW CAN I MINIMIZE MY RISK AS A PRIVATE MORTGAGE LENDER?

By following the process and fundamentals I have laid out in this book, you will be able to minimize your risks as a private mortgage lender. First, you'll want to look for win-win investing relationships by selecting investments that fit within your risk tolerance and yield expectations. Once you find potential real estate investors with the right kind of deals, be sure to perform your own due diligence by carefully researching the investor, evaluating their experience, determining their potential for success and thoroughly analyzing any potential lending opportunities.

In addition to doing your due diligence before entering into a deal, you also want to make sure that you have an experienced team to support you during the lending process. An experienced team will help you make sure you have all of the right paperwork in place to protect your investment. By structuring your loans so that you have collateral, you can still stand to gain even if the investor defaults on the loan or the investment doesn't turn out to be as profitable as you first expected.

USURY LAWS

Understanding usury is a necessary part of real estate investments. Usury is a term that means you are essentially receiving an interest rate that is higher than normal. Usury laws are state rules, so they will vary from state to state. Remember: it is the state in which the property is located.

Usury rules also change for the type of property. Real property is different from personal property. Here in Texas, the effect of usury could make a contract voidable if the lender makes a usurious loan. You always want to check local usury rules for every state, but for Texas it is 18% either contracted for, charged, or received. There can be a penalty of 3 times the excess interest, plus attorney fees. It's important to note that points collected by the lender are not part of the interest. Checking with your attorney to make sure you are not contracting a usurious note is extremely important.

SHOULD I POOL MY FUNDS WITH OTHER LENDERS?

I learned a lesson a long time ago from one of my lender's and it is this, "one lender, one lien". As a rule, I never 'pool' money to purchase a home from multiple lenders. We do of course borrow with second lien lenders, but only if we are still abiding by our acceptable loan to value ratios. So the simple rule for me is, and will continue to be one lender, one lien.

I also want to note that this conversation is a bit different from our SDIRA Investors. Meaning, often times affiliated Quest IRA clients do combine their funds together to create one lien. But this is still recognized as one lien, and in every instance, the affiliated account holders are either family or very close business associates.

FAQs about SDIRA Lending and Quest IRA

I have been working with clients for over 10 years and I am also a Quest client myself, so with the help of Nathan Long, we've included some FAQ's specifically about Quest IRA and SDIRA investing.

WHAT ARE THE DIFFERENT WAYS I CAN FUND MY SELF-DIRECTED IRA?

Rollover/Direct Rollover: Rollovers can be done from employer plans or other IRAs. To avoid taxes or penalties, make sure the rollover is done within 60 days from the time you took the distribution.

Transfer: Transfers are done when moving funds between like accounts. If you have an existing IRA at a different custodian, Quest can move the funds (cash and privately held assets) via transfer.

Deposit: Your IRA can be funded via annual contributions.

HOW CAN I TAKE FUNDS OUT OF MY IRA TO PURCHASE REAL ESTATE WITHOUT HAVING TO PAY TAXES AND PENALTIES?

When using your IRA for the purposes of purchasing Real Estate, you are not actually taking the funds out. Similar to how your IRA can purchase an asset or a stock, your IRA can also purchase an asset of Real Estate. Quest IRA specializes in helping their clients purchase real estate through their retirement accounts.

WHAT ARE THE DIFFERENCES BETWEEN BUYING REAL ESTATE PERSONALLY AND BUYING REAL ESTATE WITH MY SELF-DIRECTED IRA?

Title of the property: When using your IRA for real estate investments it must be titled in the name of your IRA. When using a Quest IRA, the title will read "Quest IRA, Inc. FBO (Your Name) IRA (Account number)."

Funds: When your IRA is used to purchase an asset, the funds must come from the IRA. This includes any expenses that are related to the investment. Likewise, any gains or earnings must go back to the IRA.

Signatures: Because investments are made in the name of the IRA, Quest IRA is actually the one that signs the documents, with your expressed and written consent of course.

CAN MY IRA BUY REAL ESTATE WITH A LOAN OR TAKE OVER A PROPERTY SUBJECT-TO AN EXISTING LOAN?

Yes. An IRA may borrow money to acquire real estate or take over a property subject to an existing loan, provided the loan is non-recourse to the IRA and to any "disqualified person." This means that typically the lender may only foreclose on the property in the event of a default. Even if there is a deficiency, the lender cannot come after the rest of the IRA's assets, nor can the lender come after the IRA owner or any other disqualified person. Neither the IRA holder nor any other disqualified person is permitted to sign a personal guarantee of the debt.

WHERE CAN I GET A NON-RECOURSE LOAN FOR MY IRA?

There are at least four sources for financing which do not violate the non-recourse requirements for IRAs. First, there is seller financing. Most sellers understand that if the loan goes into default they get the property back anyway, so asking for the loan to be non-recourse should not be too difficult to negotiate.

Second, there is private financing from financial friends. If you cultivate a reputation as a professional real estate investor, there should be no reason that your financial friends would not loan to your IRA money on a non-recourse basis, either from their own funds or from their own IRAs. I have seen IRAs borrow the money for both the purchase and the rehab on a non-recourse loan!

Third, there are banks and hard money lenders. Non-recourse loans are not the norm, so many banks will turn you down. However, there is at least one bank that lends in all 50 states, and in Houston I have seen at least 3 local banks and 2 hard money lenders make non-recourse loans to IRAs.

Finally, as mentioned above, you could take over a property subject to an existing loan, provided the originator of the loan is not you or another disqualified person.

CAN I LIVE IN OR WORK ON A HOUSE MY IRA OWNS?

No, this would be considered a prohibited transaction.

How can I work with Quest IRA?

The first step in working with Quest IRA is to speak with one of their IRA Specialists, who can help you better understand your options for taking control of your retirement with a self-directed IRA. Opening an account is simple, and they offer a variety of options, including traditional, ROTH, SEP, and SIMPLE IRAs as well as Coverdell Education Savings Accounts (ESAs), Health Savings Accounts (HSAs), and Solo 401ks.

All they require to get started is for the client to open an account, which includes a signed and dated application, signed and dated fee schedule, and copy of a valid government issued photo ID. It's important to note that Quest does not require any account minimums. If you would like more information on Quest IRA and how they help individuals make the most of their retirement investments, visit www.QuestIRA.com.

What are the typical fees at Quest?

The average fees at Quest are about $400 per deal. All of the typical fees involved in working with Quest can be located on the Quest website, just go to QuestIRA.com and search for 'Fee Schedule'. By the way, Quest will never charge for money coming into Quest in the form of a new account deposit, for example. Fees are only incurred when money goes out, with a loan being the obvious example. Quest also give their clients different options based on their investment choices. However, if money is not invested, you merely pay $25 per quarter. It should be noted when you are investing as a note investor, the borrower will typically, if not always, pay the transaction and wire fees.

Chapter 17: Closing Thoughts

"There are those who see an opportunity, and then there are those who seize an opportunity"

– Joanie Warren

Over the years I have worked with many private lenders in a few different capacities. Primarily, as a borrower completing hundreds of real estate transactions over the last decade. I have also started lending several years ago and I am increasing my lending activity each year. I've also worked as a coach and consultant to many lenders who are simply trying to make sure they are on the right path in their lending pursuits. My goal in creating this book is to help those interested in becoming private mortgage lenders get started on the right foot by providing a comprehensive overview of the lending process as well as breaking down the most successful way to structure private loans to reduce lender risk.

In this closing chapter, I'd like to go over some Chapter Takeaways that you should keep in mind as you start or continue your journey as a private mortgage lender. Most of these points have already been addressed in earlier chapters, but I feel that the information is too important not to reiterate just one more time.

UNDERSTAND WHAT YOU ARE INVESTING IN

I've said it before, and I'll say it again, it's imperative that you understand what you are investing in. Not all properties or types of investments are the same. If you want to be a successful investor, you will need to learn about the property types you're investing in. This will take some time and research on your part, but in the end, you will be glad you took the time to understand the types of investment properties you are investing in with your money.

Most private mortgage lenders specialize in a particular type of investment. Some lenders prefer to specialize in private loans for single-family homes like flips or rentals. While other lenders like to work on deals involving commercial properties. Part of the reason for this specialization is that it allows lenders to really get to know the ins and outs of a property and investment type. This can help lenders better evaluate potential deals as well as anticipate and resolve any issues that may arise.

Even if you plan on eventually investing in different types of properties, it's best to start with those that are easy to understand. The reason I recommend new private lenders to start with single-family homes is these types of investments are fairly straight forward and easy to navigate. By starting off with simpler investments, you can set yourself up for success in the very beginning. You can always move on to different types of investments, or you may just continue investing in the same type of investment for years or decades to follow.

Don't invest in any deal you don't feel comfortable with

This is important. As a private mortgage lender, you are going to be putting your hard earned capital on the line. If you don't feel comfortable investing in a deal or investing with a particular borrower, then trust your gut and don't do it. Period. There is no reason to risk your investment capital if you have any concerns or uneasy feelings about a deal. Remember, it's not a good investment if you can't sleep well at night.

There are many reasons why a lender may not feel comfortable with a deal. Perhaps a family member or friend is asking for a loan, but they have never invested before. Maybe you feel like you don't know enough about the type of investment to successfully evaluate a potential deal, or you are not confident in the real estate investor's abilities to complete the deal successfully or perhaps there is an unfavorable market condition that concerns you. No matter what the reason, you should never enter into a deal with which you're not comfortable. Deals come and go, but peace of mind is priceless.

BUILD A TEAM TO HELP YOU UNDERSTAND AND INVEST SAFELY

Private money lending is not the type of investment you should tackle alone. One of your most important assets as a private money lender is your team. You need to have a team of qualified professionals, like a real estate attorney and a title company, to help you understand each aspect of the deal and protect your investment every step of the way. Your team should be compiled of experienced individuals who can provide guidance while helping you secure your investment.

Building your team takes a little time and research. You not only want to find people who are experienced in working with the types of deals that you plan to invest in, but also people who you can trust. Your team will support you throughout your investing journey, so it is worthwhile to do your research and take the time to get to know those who will be on your team.

ONLY WORK WITH PEOPLE YOU TRUST, AND DEMAND PROPER DOCUMENTATION

Trust is an important part of the foundation of every successful real estate deal. If you cannot trust the real estate investors you are lending money to, then you will never feel comfortable investing as a private money lender. Though it can be difficult to trust someone when your personal capital is at stake in a deal, it is vital that you work to build relationships with investors and only work with those you can trust.

It takes a while to build trust, and as you work with investors, you will start to build and strengthen your relationships over time. For instance, my company has a number of private money lenders who continue to work with us time and time again because we have proven to be professionals who are capable of successful deals. We have not only proven our abilities as investors, but we have worked to build trusting relationships with our private lenders. The more we work with these lenders, the more trust we are able to build to help ensure our lenders are confident in our ability to follow through on deals.

When you are first getting started, you won't have a history with your investors. Therefore, it's important to research your investors and meet with them in person, if possible, to get a feel for whether or not you can trust them. This is when referrals or references come in handy. If someone has referred an investor to you, this is a good sign the person is someone you can trust, but of course you will still need to perform your due diligence. If the investor has references, talk to them to make sure he or she is someone you can trust.

TAKE A CONSERVATIVE APPROACH

Though it can be easy to get caught up in the excitement of investing, as a new private mortgage lender, you should take a conservative approach to lending. Be sure to leave plenty of liquidity in your personal finances so that you can handle any unexpected personal circumstances that might arise. The last thing you want to do is pour all of your money into investing while your personal finances suffer. It is much easier to invest your money in a deal than to get it back when you need it. So, consider how much money you can safely invest before entering into any deal.

As you learn more about investing and find out what works best for you, you can then adjust your strategy to account for your risk tolerance and investment goals. However, it's best to start off conservatively until you are confident in your abilities as an investor. Just like a person who has just learned to ride a bike should not participate in the Tour de France, someone who has just learned to invest with private mortgage loans should not go all in and risk all of their personal capital on their first few private mortgage loans.

REMEMBER THE STORY OF THE TORTOISE AND THE HARE

As you embark on your journey as a private mortgage lender, remember the story of the tortoise and the hare. Slow and steady wins the race. The same is true for investing. Though it may be easy to get caught up in the idea of making lots of money quickly through short-term loans with higher interest rates, this type of investing is not always sustainable in the long-term.

Most investors are looking to participate in investments that will help them build long-term wealth rather than just cash in on a quick deal. Any time you are tempted to take the easy way out when it comes to investing, consider what you can gain in the long-term by putting your money to work over a longer period of time. After all, investing is a marathon, not a sprint.

START TAKING ACTION TODAY!

There's a saying I like to use when speaking with and coaching new investors – "Nothing happens if nothing happens." My goal with this book was to provide you with a lot of valuable content and helpful information about private mortgage lending. But if you do nothing with this information then what good is it really?

My hope is the information provided in this book will empower you as a new private lender to start making your money work for you. I encourage each and every one of you to apply what you have learned in this book and start taking action. Go out and find active real estate investors and borrowers in your area. Make use of the information provided within this book to make sure you perform the proper due diligence when analyzing deals and borrowers. The knowledge you've gained from this book can help you make wise decisions and move forward in growing your net worth through private mortgage lending. And if you ever feel stuck and need help with a deal, or simply getting your lending ventures off the ground, I'm only a 'click' away, you can also contact me at www.PrivateMoneyPlaybook.com.

About Brant Phillips

Brant is a full-time real estate investor, business owner, business coach, speaker and bestselling author. He has been featured by the local media as a Real Estate expert and hosts local seminars and training events.

Brant is a proverbial 'rags to riches' story, while living in an apartment and having no money, he was able to purchase his first investment property on a credit card. He went on to by 10 properties that same year with no money down and since that time has gone on to purchase, renovate, flip and rent hundreds of homes and owns a portfolio of rental properties in the millions and continues to flip houses and take part in a variety of real estate projects, including new home construction and commercial developments.

Brant's real estate deals are almost exclusively funded from his network of Private Lenders. Many of which, Brant has worked with for close to a decade, and he is proud to call many of his lenders his closest friends. Brant is also active as a private lender himself in the Texas market.

In addition to Brant's real estate pursuits, he's an active entrepreneur as owner of a coaching and consulting business and other business ventures. One of his companies, Invest Home Pro, was recognized by Inc. 5000 as one of America's Fastest-Growing Private Companies. He is a licensed real estate agent with EXP Realty and hosts a real estate investment bootcamps called Wealth Passage.

Brant can be routinely found speaking at various networking events about real estate investing and he speaks monthly at Quest IRA teaching others how to invest passively as a private mortgage lender. He has also written several books, *How To Flip A House* and *Conversation With A Millionaire Real Estate Investor* are his most popular books in the real estate investing community.

Brant has a criminal justice degree and served seven years as police officer and prides himself on integrity and serving others. He enjoys helping and teaching people to experience the freedom and success he has achieved through successfully investing in real estate. Most importantly, Brant is a devoted husband and father of five wonderful children that inspire him to continue pursuing greatness and leading by example.

Be sure to visit the
Private Lender Playbook page
to access valuable tools & resources

www.PrivateLenderPlaybook.com

Made in the USA
Las Vegas, NV
12 July 2021